HAWAIIAN ALMANAC

Clarice B. Taylor
Illustrations by Mary Laune Aiken

MUTUAL PUBLISHING

Library of Congress Catalog Card Number: 95-81197

Cover design by Jane Hopkins
Cover photo courtesy of the Baker-Van Dyke Collection

First Printing, November 1995
Second Printing, August 1997
0 1 2 3 4 5 6 7 8 9

ISBN 1-56647-114-1

Mutual Publishing
1127 11th Avenue, Mezz. B
Honolulu, Hawaii 96816
Telephone (808) 732-1709
Fax (808) 734-4094
email: mutual@lava.net

Printed in Australia

CONTENTS

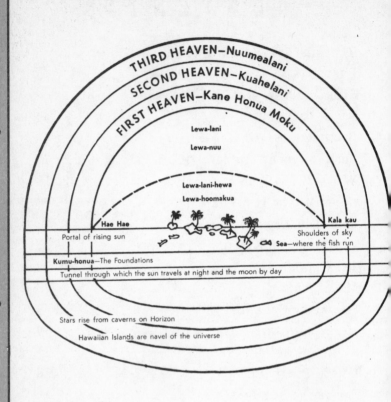

THIRD HEAVEN—Nuumealani

SECOND HEAVEN—Kuahelani

FIRST HEAVEN—Kane Honua Moku

Lewa-lani

Lewa-nuu

Lewa-lani-hewa

Lewa-hoomakua

Hae Hae

Kala kau

Portal of rising sun

Shoulders of sky

Sea—where the fish run

Kumu-honua—The Foundations

Tunnel through which the sun travels at night and the moon by day

Stars rise from caverns on Horizon

Hawaiian Islands are navel of the universe

Clarice B. Taylor became interested in the folklore of the Hawaiians during a residence of 25 years on the Island of Kauai. She became a serious student of Hawaiiana when she began compiling material for a daily column which has been appearing in the Honolulu Star-Bulletin for more than ten years.

For material in this book she has consulted living Hawaiian authorities, and has obtained material from little-known and out-of-print publications by the Bernice Pauahi Bishop Museum. Her interest in the Hawaiian Moon Calendar was encouraged by the late Sir Peter Buck, one of the world's outstanding authorities on Polynesia and former director of the Museum.

TIMEKEEPERS
OF OLD HAWAII

The Hawaiian of two centuries ago had no watch to pull out of his pocket when he wanted to determine the time to go fishing. He had no tide table to tell him when the water would be low on the reefs. He had no calendar to tell him the phase of the moon.

He depended upon man's oldest timekeepers, the stars, the moon and the sun. He had an intimate and friendly acquaintance with the heavenly timekeepers. He thought of them as gods, interested in his welfare and that of the earth on which he lived.

This bit of earth, the Hawaiian Islands, was in his opinion the center of the universe. He called the Islands navel of the universe. In fact, he located that center on the Island of Oahu at about the site of the present water pumping station on Beretania and Alapai streets.

The heavens he believed to be resting upon the "shoulders" of the horizon in three great domes, one over the other. Each dome was the heavenly home of a great god and his people.

The earth and its oceans were flat, he thought. He pictured a great passage or tunnel under the earth through which the sun traveled at night to rise again in the east in the morning

The Heavens were supported on pillars and there were proper openings through which the sun entered in the morning and set at night.

The portals through which the sun rose were poetically called *Hae-Hae*, rent asunder, and the Hawaiian said the curtains of night were parted at the coming of the sun. The western portals were called *Kalakau*, the sun lodged, and the sunset was poetically described as the sun resting on the ocean.

The Hawaiian language is rich in names used to describe the heavens and the sky.

The space directly above the earth (where a man's body would hang were he suspended from a tree with his feet off the ground) was called *lewa-hoomakua*, parent-air. The space above the tree tops was called *lewa-lani-lewa,* floating heavens. The space where the birds fly is called *lewa-nuu,* upper heavens, and the space above (where the clouds float) is *lewa-lani,* heavens that cannot be seen with the eye. *Lewa-lani,* in the Hawaiian mind, is a space directly below the heavens in which the gods live, the stars are sprinkled and the sun and moon travel.

The heavens were connected with earth by a great cloud driven about the sky by the winds and periodically visiting earth. This cloud was called *Kane-huna-moku,* or the God *Kane's* Hidden Land.

The three heavens were also described and given names. The gods who lived in them, their retainers and family members were told of and the life they lived was described.

Under the earth's foundations was a great subterranean place of dim light ruled by a god called *Milo.* This was the destination of souls who did not deserve to go straight to heaven. They lived a dull life without love or affection, eating butterflies and insects. Some of these souls were taken to heaven after a period of time in which they were purified.

Conch shell

Never expose the bones of the ones who are gone or bring them out into the sun. (Never speak evil of the dead).

* * *

To keep spirits away from the house, place bamboo sticks—the width of the door—over the door. If spirits attempt to enter they are caught in the hollow bamboo and can't get out.

PORTENTS AND SIGNS

Suppose a man is resting under a tree. He watches a spider spinning its web. Suppose the spider suddenly drops to the ground immediately in front of the man. An interpreter would tell the man that some great benefit is coming to him or that a stranger is approaching.

If the spider had dropped to the right or the left of the man, then the spider had no meaning. There would be no benefits arriving.

Suppose a woman has a twitching of the eyes and asked an interpreter the reason. She would be told that the twitching either indicates the arrival of a stranger or wailing for the dead. Her eyes would twitch with the wailing of greeting, if the stranger arrived or they would twitch with mourning for the dead.

If the twitching continued several days, perhaps ten or more, then the portent was sure to be fulfilled.

Ringing in the ears is a sign of several things and requires the interpretation of a priest to arrive at the correct reason.

Ringing in the ear generally portends that the person is being talked about and spoken ill of. If the ringing were in the right ear, then the talk was malicious and evil and was coming from a man. If the ringing were in the left ear, the malicious talk was coming from a woman. On the other hand, ringing in the ear might be an indication that the person was going to be sick.

Bristling of the hair is also an indication that the person is being talked about and not in a friendly manner. If the person were simply idling about with a feeling of contentment and suddenly felt a "bristling up of the head" then he knew that some gossip was talking about him.

On the other hand, bristling up of the head might simply be fear brought on by the sudden remembrance of a dead person.

Throbbing of the feet is a portent of two things. The throbbing might indicate that the person is moving to another locality at an unexpected time.

However, if the move does not occur, then the throbbing of the feet means that a stranger is about to visit.

STORY OF THE STARS

The Hawaiian needed no astronomical chart to locate the stars. He knew the appearance of the heavens each night of the year as people today know the face of the clock. In his dictionary, the stars included the sun, the moon and the moveable and immoveable stars. The sun he called the Great star of *Kane*. The stars he called the Innumerable Stars of *Kane*.

His religion taught him that *Kane* created the universe, the stars and mankind. The stars, the moon and the sun were his calendar. The stars had been flung into the sky by *Kane* and were then regulated by another god so that they would not stray from their path and would keep the seasons straight.

The stars were important for they were the guiding light by which mariners made long voyages, many thousands of miles, across the ocean.

The stars rose from pits along the horizon, traveled a definite course and then sank into assigned pits. The Hawaiian knew the location of the pits and the course of the stars, and could navigate by them. Certain stars "hung over each island" and it was by the location of those stars that the mariner knew he was approaching land.

In the Bishop Museum there is a gourd on which a Hawaiian instructor in navigation marked the lines which guide a mariner. He first located *Kiopaa*, the North Star, and then *Newa*, the Southern Star. He drew a line between the two stars and so divided his sky in two parts.

The much Traveled Path of *Kanaloa* (*Ke ala nui naawe a Kanaloa*) was the region lying to the west of this line. The Bright Road of *Kane* (*Ke alaula a Kane*) was the name of the region to the left of the line.

The instructor then drew three lines from east to west across his sky. One line was roughly drawn at the equator, the other two at the equinoxes. The two lines which we think of as the equinoxes represented to the Hawaiian the travels of the sun either furthest north or south.

8

The Black Shining Road of *Kane (Ke alanui polohiwa a Kane)* was the name given the northern line and the Black Shining Road of *Kanaloa (Ke alanui polohiwa a Kanaloa)* was the name of the southern line.

In these sections of the sky, the astronomer fixed the hanging stars over their islands, the stars by which the navigator guided his canoe and the "foreign stars," those outside the main traveled routes.

In his imagination, the Hawaiian saw "the highways" of these many stars and knew their approximate time.

Mahina, the moon, was of great importance for it was by the moon that the Hawaiian fixed his monthly timetable and knew when to plant and when to fish.

The sun, "The great Star of *Kane,*" was important as a regulator of the seasons, in addition to providing warmth and regulating the growth of all things.

The Hawaiian priest provided himself with stone markers to help him ascertain the time of the year which the sun would approach the Black Shining Road of *Kane* and the time it would approach the Black Shining Road of *Kanaloa.*

At *Kumukahi,* the most easterly point of the Big Island and the entire group of Hawaiian Islands, there are standing today stone markers which denoted the seasons.

There is a story of two brothers connected with these stones. *Kumukahi* and his brother *Palamoa* were chiefs of godly wisdom who came to Hawaii from *Kahiki* (far away land). The brothers had four wives, *Kanono, Pau-poulu, Ha'eha'e* and *Hanaka-ulua.*

Kumukahi quarreled with the volcano goddess *Pele* and he and his wives were destroyed in a lava flow. The soul of *Kumukahi* entered the plover bird.

Drum

The four wives became stones and were so spaced apart to mark the southernmost journey and the northernmost journey of the sun. The two center wives marked the portals of the rising sun and the sunset.

The Hawaiian priests said that *Kanono* (southern limit) and *hanaka-ulua* (northern limit) spent their time pushing the sun back and forth to keep the seasons in their proper place. *Ha'eha'e* (eastern Portal) and *pau-poulu* (western portal) kept the entrances to the "spider's path across the sky" opened and closed. It was the spider's path which the sun climbed each day.

Similar points were marked on each of the Islands so that the Island priests, who kept the calendar, could visit them regularly to set their calculations correctly.

THE PLEIADES YEAR

The Hawaiian divided his calendar into the space of a year composed of 12 months or moons. He did not control the division of time known as a year by the sun, as we do, but by a small group of stars which we call the Pleiades and he called *Makalii* (small eyes).

There are many bright and beautiful stars with whom the Hawaiian was familiar and by which he might have regulated his calendar. Instead, he chose to regulate it by the rising and setting of this small constellation of seven stars. As a result, he considered the Pleiades the most important stars in the heavens.

Just why the Pleiades were selected as the regulator of the year is lost in antiquity. Most Asiatic, all the Pacific Island peoples and some Indian tribes use the rising and setting of the Pleiades as the regulator of the year.

The "Small Eyes" are to be seen on the eastern horizon about the middle of November each year. They travel across the sky for six months on the Black Shining Road of *Kane* and set about the middle of June in a pit located in the western sky.

The rising of Small Eyes from its eastern pit on the horizon heralds the coming of the New Year. The first month of the New Year is called *Makalii* in honor of the constellation. Priests watch faithfully for the appearance of Small Eyes and pronosticate the type of weather to be had during the coming year by its appearance.

Hawaiians did not number or name their years. It was sufficient for them to know that a year had passed. Chief purpose of dividing time into years was to regulate annual festivals such as the *Makahiki*, the great harvest festival. Age was a matter of indifference to the Hawaiian as calculated in years. He considered age by its true physical characteristics. A baby was a baby until weaned. He was then a child until puberty. At puberty he became a young man and was considered young until his hair began to whiten and he showed symptoms of old age. Old age lasted until death.

Each year had two seasons, the wet and the dry. The wet season was *hoo-ilo* and the dry was *kau*. During the dry season the sun stood directly overhead, daylight was prolonged and the trade winds blew. Both day and night were warm and vegetation grew fast.

During the *hoo-ilo* the sun declined to the south, the nights lengthened, the nights and days were cool and vegetation died away. The dry months roughly ran from May until about the middle of October. The wet season began in November and lasted until May.

Bowl

10

STARS AS GUIDES

The Innumerable stars of *Kane* were not only the Hawaiians' timekeeper, they were guardian gods and spirits of their ancestors and they helped rule the destinies of the people as well as the months.

The most dramatic use the Hawaiians made of the stars was as an aid to navigation. By following the stars, the Polynesians who became the Hawaiians traveled thousands of miles across the Pacific to discover Hawaii.

For centuries after their discovery, Hawaiians traveled back and forth to *"Kahiki"* (believed to be Tahiti) by the aid of the stars. They knew and recognized the stars which "hung over" Tahiti and the stars which "hung over" Hawaii.

Navigators selected a guiding star when they left land. The star was often at the back of the canoe. As it rose in the heavens, the navigator placed a bowl of water in front of him so that the star would shine into the water. He guided the canoe by keeping the star shining in the water. The North star and the South star were the two "fixed" stars which guided their navigation.

Much information has been lost about the Hawaiian star lore. Once Hawaiians began using watches and clocks, they forgot their star lore and no one thought to write it down.

A comparison of the names of the month with the far greater star lore known and remembered by southern Polynesians leads astronomers to believe that the months were named for their "guiding stars" and that this knowledge has largely been forgotten.

The importance of the Pleiades in fixing the year, adds support to this theory. The coming of the Pleiades, which Hawaiians called *Makalii,* was watched for with great concern.

If the Pleiades were clear and bright, then the weather would be dry and there might be a famine. If they were misty in appearance, then the season would be wet and there might be floods.

The Pleiades were the governing stars of the month of Makalii for all living things. If the weather was normal, then crops grew bountifully. If the weather was bad, it effected the crops. Fishermen watched just as earnestly, for the Pleiades told them many things

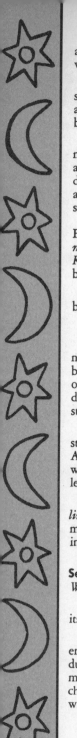

about fishing. The temperament of children born during the month was guided by the Pleiades.

KAELO (January-February) is believed to have been named for a star known as *Kaelo* in Tahiti. The Hawaiians forgot about this star and did not hand down any information about it. The star may have been the bright star in the Belt of Orion or the planet Mercury.

KAULUA (February-March) may have been the Hawaiian pronunciation for the star *Takurua* of South Polynesia. This star was Sirius and the name "slow pit" refers to the lingering of the sun at its lowest declination. Hawaiians forgot about this and adopted the star *Pauahi* as the governing star of the month. *Pauahi* was an early morning star, but no one knows just which.

But the Hawaiians remembered bits about *Kaulua* in their chants. For instance they remembered that the full name was *Kaulua-i-hai-mohai* and that it guarded the sacrifices laid upon the altars of the gods. *Kaulua* also governs those born during the month and gives them a brave disposition with violent tempers.

NANA (March-April) has no governing star which anyone remembers.

WELO (April-May) is another month whose star has been forgotten.

IKIIKI (May-June) is the month governed by a "people's star" named *Kaulia*. Hawaiians believed that the *makaaina* (commoner) born during *Ikiiki* would be fond of agriculture due to the influence of *Kaulia*. Since the Southern Cross is visible in Hawaiian skies during the month, some think Kaulia may be one of its prominent stars. Others think it may have been Mercury.

KAAONA (June-July). The governing star of this month was also named *Kaaona*. All that we know of *Kaaona* is that the star was named for a brother of *Hawaii-loa*, the legendary discoverer of the Islands.

Hula instruments

HINAIAELEELE, commonly known as *Hilinaehu* or *Hilinehu* **(July-August)** was the month governed by *Kumu-koa*, a star prominent in the morning sky.

MAHOE MUA or *Hilinama* **(August-September)** was governed by the star *Wehewehe.* Nothing is known about the star.

MAHOE-HOPE (September-October). Nothing is known about its governing star.

IKUWA (October-November) an important month, it was governed by a royal star named *Kauka-malama*. This star shone all night during the month and disappeared on the first night of the following month. Hawaiians also called the star *Kahela,* name of a feminine chief. The star was responsible for the rain, lightning, thunder, high wind and high surf which mark the month. Some said it was the husband of a chiefess who gave birth to men with loud voices and contentious dispositions.

WELEHU (November-December) is the month in which the Pleiades rise and foretell the coming of the new year. Since the star Antares is prominent during the month, the name *Welehu* is possibly a forgotten name for Antares.

MAKALI'I (December-January) was dominated by the Pleiades constellation and probably a morning star of which we know nothing. *Makalii* was probably the month in which the *Kilo* (Hawaiian astronomer) was instructed to watch the skies for omens of the coming year. The king made his plans accordingly.

There was a star called *Kane* which sometimes appeared above the moon and was visible only to the astrologers and priests. When seen, it foreboded the death of the king and he was accordingly cautioned to stay close at home and under guard.

If the king were planning a battle campaign, the astrologers watched for the conjunction of planets with certain stars and made their predictions.

Most important was the performance of a star called *Holo holo pinaau* (the traveler), which may have been Mars. It was watched to determine whether the star entered a certain circle of twelve stars, whether it drew to one side before reaching the circle or whether it traveled either to the east or the west of the circle of twelve stars.

If *Holoholopinaau* entered the circle, then disaster was certain to befall the government. Partial disasters were foretold by it's behaviour otherwise.

Haka-moa (the chicken roost) was another important star to watch. It was so important that the King often appointed one particular astronomer to be "chief of the chicken-roost."

It is bad luck to dream of gaining valued possessions and waken to reality.

* * *

You choose to cook your fish; I want to eat mine raw.

* * *

The mouths of certain people are always clacking.

* * *

It (an insult) will come back to your red mouth.

* * *

The prayer of the Kahuna (priest) is like a worm, it lies in the dust until the day it moves on.

BIRTH OMENS

Birth omens of the Hawaiian are a good indication of what traits the Hawaiian found to be desirable and what to despise. The hospitable and generous man or woman was admired above all others. If a person could be prosperous and at the same time generous and hospitable, he was most admirable.

The prosperous person who kept all his possessions and never gave them away was stingy. To be stingy was to be despicable.

An understanding of the characteristics which the Hawaiian felt to be desirable, gives an insight into why the Hawaiian has had difficulty adjusting to a competitive way of life in modern times.

Only a partial list of daily birth omens has been left us by the old Hawaiians. The incomplete list follows.

HOAKA (second day of the month). A male child born during the day will grow into a man who perpetually grumbles about getting his share, he will be a trouble maker, stingy, unmerciful and conceited. He will be clever at getting things out of others, suave but discourteous at heart. He will have some lovable qualities and will be efficient.

A woman born on *Hoaka* will be one to show her teeth, although she will conceal her temper under cover of affable ways. She will be dignified and appear unassuming, but will in reality be a hypocrite, vain and a woman always loitering about housedoors.

KUKAHI (third day). A man born on that day will be dauntless, strong, brave, unyielding, kindhearted, strong of body but always making mistakes.

A woman born on that day will be an ensnarer, of little pride and continually eating what is left over by others.

KUPAU (sixth day). The man born on that day will be one who clings to what he is taught. If he is properly taught as a boy, he will be a good man. If he has had evil teachings, he will be bad. Nothing can change the character of a man born on this day.

A woman born this day will be a virtuous woman. Her thought will be on her work and she will be ashamed to ask for anything or go about to homes of others asking favors. She will have enemies without cause and other women will find fault with her. She will be a woman who works hard and will have prosperous and good look-ing sweethearts.

OLEKUKAHI (seventh day). A man born that day will be one who is secretive about his own gains and denies them with his mouth. He gains little, is lazy, a glutton, fond of pleasure, a drunkard, grumbler, poor provider and one who is not ashamed to depend upon a woman.

He has a hard heart and will take food from the patch of a woman or from that of children. He is the kind who will loiter about the doorway at meal time. If he is taking care of a child for some one else, he will expect to be paid for it and if he is not paid will grumble. He will send children to other people's houses to ask for taro, potato and so forth.

A woman born on that day is bad tempered but will do some hands, but she will be a grumbler, quick tempered and one who forces others to work. *Olekukahi* is generally a day of bad omens.

OLEKULUA (eighth day). A man born on that day is fond of pleasure but is also a good worker.

A woman born onthat day is bad tempered but will do some work. She is talkative, a gossip, eager for praise, fond of associating with her betters, self willed, assuming to herself honor that is not her own, and one who critizes other women.

OLEKUKOLU (ninth day). A man or woman born on this day will be acquisitive, what they have they get from others. He or she will be merciless and stingy.

OLEPAU (tenth day). A man or woman born on this day will be prosperous.

HUNA (eleventh day). A man born that day will be modest, kind, hospitable, a man of wisdom. He will have enemies who plot against him and many who speak against him because of his good name.

Akua sticks

He will be despised causelessly and will be troubled by others causelessly.

A woman born on that day will become famous, but she too will be troubled by those who envy her good name.

MOHALU (twelfth day). A man born on that day will be a skeptical person with-out faith, but a good worker.

A woman born on Mohalu will be a skeptic and an indolent worker.

HUA (thirteenth day). A man or woman born on that day will be prosperous. The man will be loved by everyone, kindhearted and popular. He will be one with a famous name.

The woman will be prosperous, but she will not be loved or popular and she will not attain a famous name.

AKUA (fourteenth day). A man born on that day will be wealthy

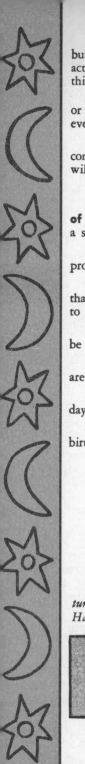

but one who has no regard for his parents. A bad hearted man, his acts will be disgraceful. He will be a spendthrift, giving away everything he has.

A woman born that day will be the same sort of person. A man or woman born during the daylight hours will be a person who loves everyone.

HOKU (fifteenth day). A man or woman born that day will become famous and rich. They will have many enemies. The woman will be very active.

These birth omens reflect the good omens of the fullmoon of Hoku.

MAHEALANI (sixteenth day and traditional full moon night of great good luck). A man or woman born on *Mahealani* will be a striver.

KULU (seventeenth day). The person born on that day will be prosperous, affectionate and loved by everyone.

LAAU KUKAHI (eighteenth day). The man or woman born on that day will be a person of fine character, eager for knowledge and to hear and know new things.

OLEKUKAHI (twenty-first day). A person born on that day will be inefficient.

OLEKULUA (twenty-second day). The birth signs for that day are of a good person, one who is modest and quiet.

KALOA KUKAHI (twenty-fourth day). The person born on that day will be a good man.

KALOA KULUA (twenty-fifth day). This is a good day for the birth signs of men.

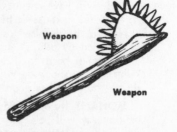

Weapon

Weapon

The plover alights on the knoll and when its breast is dark, returns to the foreign land. (Description of the foreigner who comes to Hawaii, gets rich and returns home).

BIRTH SIGNS BY THE MONTH

IKIIKI (May-June). A man born during the month of *Ikiiki* will be a man fond of farming. He will always want a great many people about him in his home, but his own family will be first in his affections.

KAAONA (June-July). Good fortune is in store for the boy born during *Kaaona*. He will be favored in all his works and sought after by women. Ruling chiefs will be his associates and he will be a great favorite among them. Hawaiians called such a person "the intoxicating shrub of *Makalei*." (*Makalei* is a shrub from which an intoxicate was made to stupify fish.)

HINAIAELEELE (July-August). The child born this month will be a lazy ignoramous, one who desires pleasures and will not apply itself to learning.

MAHOE-MUA (August-September) and **MAHOE-HOPE (September-October),** the twin months. A child born during either of the twin months will be an enigma. He will sometimes indulge in mischief and at other times be a model of good behavior. If a good deed is his first conscious act, he will do good all his life. If his first conscious act is evil, he will be mischievous all his life.

IKUWA (October-November) This child will be a person with a very loud voice, suitable for that of a herald. He will be well liked by the chiefs as a heralding officer and will be taken into the councils of the priests. His opinion will be like the clap of thunder during *Ikuwa*.

WELEHU (November-December) and **MAKALII (December-January).** Birth omens for either of these months are most auspicious. The man or woman will have many children. The family will be spoken of "as an assembly of *manini*" (small fish), or a "school of *uhu*" (large fish).

KAELO (January-February). Birth omens for this month are also very auspicious. The man or woman will be of an affectionate nature, one who holds the affections of family members and easily gains the love and regard of others. This person is charitable and will have a host of friends.

KAULUA (February-March). Like the month of *Kaulua,* in which violent storms may be expected, the child born during this month will be a mighty man in battle, brave and violent tempered. The *Kaulua* person will be called "the violent billow of *Kaulua*."

NANA (March-April). The *Nana* person can go through life assured that whatever he or she undertakes, whether it be fishing, farming or homemaking, will be successful.

WELO (April-May). The man born during *Welo* will be an illustrious person and his children will follow in his footsteps. His chief skill will be in divination and counseling.

17

WORSHIP OF GODS

HOOMANA (RELIGION)

The Hawaiian saw god in everything about him, the trees, plants, land animals, sea animals, rocks and human beings. Life in each thing was actuated by a god called *akua*. Each *akua* had a name and certain attributes.

There were four great gods in the Polynesian system of the universe—*Ku, Kane, Lono* and *Kanaloa*. Each of the four great gods had certain powers and certain duties.

Ku was called the architect and builder. He was the great god who presided over war and to whom human sacrifices were made. His worship days occurred at the beginning of the moon month and were four in succession. He had his own temples built according to certain specifications and attended by a distinct cult of priests.

Kane was the creator and giver of life. He created man with the help of *Lono*. He also created the forests, brought certain rains and life in general. He was the great healer and lived in many of the most precious healing plants. *Kane* had his own temples and his own priests. He was known by many names, depending upon the attribute of the particular god or its purpose.

Lono was the god of agriculture and peace. He was probably the best known of the great gods and the most beloved. His presence was seen in the rain clouds and in growing things. To him, the householder dedicated his family worship and made daily offerings. To him, the farmer dedicated his first fruits.

Kanaloa was the god of the great immensurable ocean and all the living things within it. Strange things happened to the worship of *Kanaloa*. In Tahitian theology, *Kanaloa* was the creator of the universe and man. By the time the Polynesians came to Hawaii he had been overthrown and was the "brother" of *Kane*.

When Christianity came to Hawaii and the Hawaiians tried to fit.

heir old religion into the teachings of the Trinity, *Kanaloa* was literally expelled from Heaven and became the devil.

In addition to these great gods, the Hawaiians worshipped thousands of other demigods and lesser gods, the more important being the volcano goddess *Pele* and her family. *Pele* was an earthbound goddess who could take on many transformations as a woman and was bound by certain powers and limitations in each transformation.

Worship of each god in old Hawaii was a religion with system. A mere human being could not know why a god was angry or was pleased. It took a priest with learning to interpret the actions of the gods. Out of this grew a definite theology complete with prayers and ceremonies to be performed in the temples.

THE MAKAHIKI

Instead of having a series of one day or one week holidays scattered throughout the year, the Hawaiian had one great harvest festival called the *Makahiki*. It lasted about three months for the majority of the people and four months for the royal court and the priests.

Three weeks of that time were given over to great sports tournaments and feasting.

The *Makahiki* was the outgrowth of the worship of *Lono,* god of fertility and peace. *Lono* was believed to have lived on earth and taught the people how to farm. When he left the earth (in a canoe) he promised to return. Each year the priests of *Lono* looked forward to the return of their god. In his absence they prepared a great banner which looked like a seventeen foot sail. They decorated the banner and placed a small image of Lono at the top.

The *Makahiki* was declared in October of each fall. It came at the close of the harvest. It was timed to dispose of the surplus foods. Food could not be kept in storage in this warm climate. The temples of the god *Ku* were closed and all life was declared dedicated to *Lono*. A herald went about proclaiming the law of *Lono*. There was to be no war, no work, no fishing and no fighting during the *Makahiki*.

On the first day of the festival the priests of *Lono* started a journey around the island carrying the banner of the god. That was the signal for everyone to pay their taxes in foodstuff, feathers and artifacts. *Lono* blessed the piles of taxes, released the land and marched on until he had made the full circuit of the island. As soon as the land was released, the people gathered for fun.

Poi pounder

They ate up the food paid in taxes. The King and court had the first share, the priests the next and the lesser chiefs the next portion. Great sports tournaments took place in each district on the island followed by hula dancing.

Farmers enjoyed the festival for about three weeks and then went back to work growing the next crop. Fishermen went back to sea at the end of the festivities and caught the fish needed for the ceremonies which brought good luck to the fishermen all the following year.

During the fourth month of the *Makahiki*, the King and the priests held a series of important ceremonies. They bade farewell to *Lono* by setting a canoe adrift in which there were enough foodstuffs to last the god until he reached *Kahiki*.

Other ceremonies were performed to bring fertility to the soil and good crops. Final rituals purified the King and all the people so that they could go back to the regular worship of the gods. At the end of the four months, the taboo on war was lifted.

Spear rack

COUNTING IN HAWAIIAN

1. kahi	6. ono
2. lua	7. hiku
3. kolu	8. walu
4. ha	9. iwa
5. lima	10. umi

11. **umikumamakahi** (*umi*, 10, *kumama*, and, *kahi*, one).
12. **umikumamalua** (*umi*, 10, *kumama*, and, *lua*, 2) etc.

20. **iwakalua**. 21. **iwakaluakumama kahi** (*iwakalua*, 20, *kumama*, and, *kahi*, 1) etc.

30. **kanakolu**. 31. **kanakolu kumama kahi** (*kanakolu*, 30, *kumama*, and, *kahi*, 1) etc.

40. **kanaha**. After 40, the Hawaiian started counting from one until he reached 50.

50. **kanaha me ka umi** (40 and 10). 60. **akahi kanaha me ka iwakalua** (40 and 20). 80. **elua kanaha** (two 40s). 100. **elua kanaha me ka iwakalua** (two 40s and 20). 600. **hookahi lau a me na kanaha elima** (one 400 and five 40s). 10,000. **Alua mano me na lau elima** (two 4000s and five 400s).

Beyond this number the Hawaiian used the term **nalowale** which means out of sight.

LOVE INDUCING

A man or woman in love could always get help when their own efforts as a suitor failed. Help came from a special class of priests who lived in old Hawaii. These priests practised the art of "love inducing."

A man might take a bit of the clothing, the hair or a finger nail clipping from the object of his affections and ask the priest to pray over them and induce love.

A man in love with a woman who lived at a distance might never have had the courage to tell the woman of his love. He would take a joint of the sugar cane called *Manu Lele,* flying bird, to the priest and ask the priest to pray over it. The flying bird cane would cause the words of the priest to fly to the woman and induce her love. The lover would then call on the woman confident that she would return his affections.

Sometimes the words of the priest were so effective that the priest could predict that the woman herself would come to her lover. Some powerful priests could even predict the time of her arrival.

A woman suspicious of her husband's faithfulness would take a joint of the sugar cane called *papa'a,* hold fast, to the priest and ask him to cast a spell over her husband so that his love for her would "hold fast." After the prayers had been said, the woman took the sugar cane home and fed it to her husband.

A husband who suspected that another love inducing priest had cast a spell over his wife would take a joint of the sugar cane called *Lau Kona* to a priest and ask to have the work of the first priest "unloosened." The efficacy of the priests' prayer was strengthened by the name of the sugar cane. *Lau* means leaf and *Kona* means the gusty southerly wind. The leaf was a beautiful green and white stripe.

The *Kona* wind would blow the first priests "love work" away when eaten by the wife. In other words, the priest would "unloosen the love work" with the *Lau Kona.*

A young girl being courted by a man would take two *ilima* blossoms to the priests to learn whether or not the man's love would be permanent. The priest would place a bowl of clear water on the prayer mat in front of the girl. He would then place the *ilima* blossoms in the water and pray. If the *ilima* came together and stayed together, the priest predicted an enduring love and advised the girl to say "yes."

If the blossoms came together for a time and then floated apart, the priest would advise the girl to say "no," since the love was only an infatuation.

Many girls were saved from bad marriages by the priest. When troubled married folks came to the priest for help, the priest would often cast lots to gain an augury before he would accept the case.

Sometimes the lots were cast by drawing pebbles from a basket. The priest would place the basket in front of the applicant and tell him or her to alternate with him in drawing pebbles from it. If the priest drew the last pebble, he knew that his work would be effective. If the applicant drew the last pebble, the priest refused to take the case. He would prophecy that the rift between husband and wife would never be healed.

Induced love brought a great change in the character of the person affected. The person went about with a fixed look in the eye, thought of no one but the beloved and talked of nothing but the beloved.

Hair necklace

When the shoals are full of fish, the birds will alight on the beach. (Where there is food, people will gather).

* * *

His teeth are yellow with wisdom.

* * *

Like the wind that goes one way and comes back, the mind also turns and thought departs. (One forgets a promise when convenient).

* * *

Let not the inexperienced sail out in a storm, lest he die in the ocean and his dead body float ashore.

* * *

Were you the one standing there and holding the towel?
(Asked of one who casts disparaging remarks upon the paternity of a child).

THE MOON MONTH

Mahina, the moon, was the goddess who kept time for the Hawaiian. *Mahina* was more important to everyday life than the sun or the stars.

The rising and the setting of the moon marked a day for the Hawaiian only he did not call the time a day, he called it a night. The appearance of the new moon and the death of the old moon marked the month for the Hawaiian, which he called *Mahina.* Twelve such moons made a year for him.

The importance of knowing the passing of a year was to know when to celebrate the *Makahiki,* the great harvest festival. It was important to know just when the festival should be celebrated because it coincided with the coming of the god *Lono* on a visit to each district in the Islands.

It was the duty of certain priests trained as astronomers to keep the annual calendar and watch the moon to determine just when certain *tabu* should be placed on the fish or land.

A proper planting season for the farmer depended upon the time as announced by the astronomer. The bird catcher, the canoe builder and many other craftsmen depended upon the astronomer's announcement of the correct *Mahina.*

Each moon had a name which helped the commoner regulate his life. Originally these names are believed to have been derived from the name of the star which guided the moon. But the commoner forgot the star names and interpreted the moon names as they applied to the ordinary things of life.

Almost anyone can keep a moon calendar according to the laws followed by the astronomer of old. First buy a calendar printed by an Island firm. This is important because the Hawaiian calendar will give the correct time of the new moon as it occurs in Hawaii. A

mainland calendar will not do because the moon appearances vary as much as twenty-four hours.

The new moon night of the modern Hawaiian calendar was the dark night of the ancient Hawaiian and the last night of the old moon.

The new moon of the Hawaiian was the first night on which the new moon was seen in the western sky. The modern may locate it by specifying the second night of the new moon on the modern calendar as the first night of the old. Counting the first night, the moon then runs either twenty-nine or thirty days until the next "new moon."

In attempting to keep an ancient moon calendar, it is essential to know when to correct the moon calendar so that the seasons will correspond with the sun. That is the secret of the ancient astronomer which we do not know. King Kalakaua said the astronomer corrected his calendar by adding five bonus days at the end of the *Makahiki* each year.

Other old Hawaiians say that the astronomer simply knew when to add extra days or an extra month. Apparently astronomers on the different Islands and in the different districts had various methods of adjusting the calendar because we know that the names of the months varied on each Island. Modern astronomers who have studied the problem believe that the Hawaiian astronomers had a system similar to that of the old Greeks by which they readjusted their calendar every nineteen years.

MAKALI'I (December-January) was the first month of the New Year. It was timed by the appearance of the Pleiades in the eastern sky. *Makali'i* began with the first new moon after the rising of the Pleiades, and was the Hawaiian name for the Pleiades, but the commoner interpreted the name as meaning "Little Eyes" for the shoots which he saw growing on the yams and arrowroot.

Makali'i occurs during the wet season. The inside stalk of the tree fern begins to grow firm and sweet and was relished as an appetizer. During this period the rats leave the cold forests and descend to the warm plains.

In most districts purification ceremonies were being performed by the priests and King as an ending to the riotous festival of the *Makahiki*. The object of these ceremonies was to purify the land and the people so that luxuriant crops might be grown in the new year. Kona winds (south winds) prevail during *Makali'i*.

Calabash

KAELO (January-February). *Ka* (the) *elo*, (drenching time) is the second month of the year. Food plants are watersoaked (another meaning of the word *Kaelo*) during the month. Southerly winds culminate and gradually give way to the northerly winds. Migrating birds are fat and good to eat. *Kaelo* is the month in which the farmer watches for *enuhe,* the worm which chews up the leaves of the green plants.

KAULUA (February-March) is the moon of "two minds." *Ka,* (the), *ulua* (double), was the translation given the name by the people. It is a month of alternating warm and cold winds. The weather is undecided and so makes the people undecided whether to go to the mountains, stay indoors or go to the sea shore. It is the moon during which fledgling birds cheep as they begin to feather out. The *Lehua* and *ohia* begin to blossom in the lower forests so the bird catchers prepare their nets and snares and journey into the forests to set up temporary houses for the birdcatching season.

NANA (March-April) is the month of living in warmth. Every living thing, whether a plant, bird of living being, shows animation during this moon. Mother birds are busy feeding their fledglings which try to get out of the nest. *Lehua* and *ohia* are blossoming so that the bird catcher sets his traps about these beautiful trees.

WELO (April-May) is the moon in which "tails stand on edge" and a man see things thrive. It is the great month for the farmer, one of the most productive of the year. The bird catcher sees the *ohia* trees send out fresh leaves and its blossoms give way to growth of fruit.

IKI'IKI (May-June) is the warm and sticky moon during which there is little wind. It is the humid beginning of the real hot weather when crops are maturing, food is plentiful and everyone yearns to go fishing. Some said that *Iki'iki* means "enough" because men and crops have enough sunshine. In this month, the people rejoice in the first breadfruit of the season.

The rats have left the plains and have returned to the mountains where they pounce upon the fern fronds.

The *lehua* begins blossoming in the highest forests and the bird catchers begin their second season's work. Mountain apples have burst forth in the lower forest areas and the birds follow to the highlands where they feed on the blossoming *lehua.*

KA'AONA (June-July) is the moon which pleasantly rolls along. *Ka'a* are the pretty puffy clouds, *ona* is pleasant or beautiful. This is a happy moon month. Food is plentiful, everyone can turn to fishing. It is a most fortunate month in which to marry, to build a new house or a canoe. Marriages made in *Ka'aona* will be happy and produce many strong children.

HINAIA'ELE'ELE (July-August) is the moon of the dark clouds which cling to the mountains. *Ele'ele* (dark), *Hina ia* (clinging to the mountains). This is the moon of the hot weather season in which there are sudden showers. The sky is full of dark clouds and plants are weighted down with ripening fruits. This is the month when the women and children love to go into the cool forests and pick the ripening mountain apples.

MAHOE MUA (August-September) is the first of the twin moons.

Mahoe Mua and *Mahoe Hope* (the month to follow) are as alike as twins. Rain and wind alternate with hot sunshine. Rough seas alternate with smooth. It is the first month of the rainy season.

MAHOE HOPE (September-October) is the second twin *mahina* of the rainy season. It is the month to complete stores for the winter, to search out the roots of the wild food plants in the forests and to prepare for the coming *Makahiki*.

IKUWA (October-November) the *mahina* of the *konohiki*, so called because of the heralds of the *konohiki* (district chief) go about the land calling with a loud voice for all to bring their taxes and first fruits to him. *Ikuwa* means "loud voice" for there is thunder in the skies, wind in the lowlands and crashing surf at the seashore. Bird catchers come down from the mountains with their season's catch and either give their feathers to the *konohiki* or trade them for food stores.

Everyone spends much of this time playing in the surf.

WELEHU (November-December) is the *mahina* of fun, the month of the *Makahiki* when all turn to the worship of the god *Lono* who brings fertility and peace. The temples of the dread gods *Ku, Kane* and *Kanaloa* are closed—only those of *Lono* are open. War is forbidden—work is forbidden—fighting is forbidden. The populace follows the god *Lono* as he makes a circuit of the district, blessing the taxes. Then all turn to sports and pleasures for the *Makahiki* season.

The following table shows how the names of the months varied on each Island, a result of the different methods the astronomer priest used to calculate days and months.

OAHU	MOLOKAI	HAWAII
Nana	Ikuwa	Makali'i
Welo	Hinaiaeleele	Kaelo
Ikiiki	Welo	Kaulua
Kaaona	Makalii	Nana
Hinaiaeleele	Kaelo	Welo
Mahoe Mua	Kaulua	Ikiiki
Mahoe Hope	Nana	Kaanao
Ikuwa	Ikiiki	Hinaiaeleele
Welehu	Kaaona	Mahoe Mua
Makalii	Hilinaehu	Mahoe Hope
Kaelo	Hilinama	Ikuwa
Kaulua	Welehu	Welehu

KAUAI	MAUI
Hilioholo	Ikuwa
Hilionalu	Welehu
Hukipau	Makalii
Ikuwa	Kaelo
Welehu	Kaulua
Kaelo	Nana
Ikiiki	Welo
Hinaiaeleele	Ikiiki
Mahoe Mua	Kaaona
Mahoe Hope	Hinaiaeleele
Hilinama	Hilinehu
Hilinehu	Hilinama

The name *Hilinaehu,* used on Islands other than Hawaii, refers to the mists (*ehu*) which float up from the sea. *Hilinama* was so called because it was necessary to keep the canoes well lashed (*hili*).

TAPA MAKING

The Hawaiians clothed themselves in a cloth made from the inner fibers of the bark of a tree. They knew no weaving, but they developed a high technique for the making of paper cloth.

The cloth was so common that articles made from it were thrown away or burned when soiled. The Hawaiian wife did not have to cope with a weekly washing.

A tree called the *wauke* in Hawaiian and known in English as the paper mulberry was grown for the express purpose of making cloth. It grew in moist upland places and was planted in large patches and cultivated so that the slender trunks of the saplings grew straight and tall.

During the slack planting season each year, parties were formed to go into the uplands and cut the *wauke*. Men did this work.

Bark was stripped from the *wauke* plant in lengths about two inches wide and six feet long. The process of making the bark into cloth was begun at the site. Each strip of bark was "softened" by placing it in a stream of running water weighted down with a rock.

Women then took over the work. The softened bark was placed on a flat board and the bark scraped off with a shell, leaving the inner bark fibers from which the cloth was made.

The clean fibers were again soaked in water, sometimes at the site of the *wauke* plantation and sometimes at the home site where women had a *lanai* or shed under which they worked on the *tapa*.

When properly softened, the fibre mass was transferred to a smooth stone where it was pounded into a felt with either a stone or a wooden paddle. The felt mass was again soaked until ready for the final beating. This was done on a wooden anvil with a wooden paddle. Plain paddles were used to beat the mass out into sheets the required width and length of the garment for which the *tapa* was wanted.

While still wet, the sheet of material was printed with geometric patterns by using paddles on which the pattern had been carved. Sometimes the sheet was dyed with vegetable coloring and then printed. The tapa was completed when laid out to dry.

The wives of the artisans and farmers made the plain *tapas*. Rich, decorated *tapas* were made by the wives of the chiefs. The chiefesses took pride in making beautiful designs and gave each design a name. The work of a certain chiefess could often be told by the design printed on the *tapa*.

MOON NIGHTS

The moon, *mahina,* was the Hawaiians' most important time-keeper because the moon not only divided the year into months, but divided the month into days. The time in which the moon traveled the skies from its rising in the west until the night of darkness set the number of days in the month. The rising of the moon in the evening until the setting of the moon in the morning established the night. Hawaiians did not think of calculating "days," they calculated nights.

Some thought of the period of time which we call a day as the time between noon, "when the sun stood overhead," until midnight "when the fish turn in the milky way." Others thought of the twenty-four hour period as the time from the setting of the sun to the setting of the next sun.

The Hawaiian did not divide the twenty-four hour night into hours and minutes. That is probably why he has such difficulty in conceiving of the length of a minute or an hour today.

He spoke of morning as "the rising of the sun." Noon was the time when the sun "stood overhead." Afternoon was the time when the "sun turned toward the west." Evening was the time when the sun set. Evening was also the time when the evening star appeared in the west. At midnight, the fishes turn in the milky way. Early morning was the time the morning star shone brightly.

The nights of the Hawaiian were regulated by the phases of the moon which he considered were three and not four as we do. The moon grew large, it rounded and it waned. The nights were named for these phases of the moon. Each phase roughly corresponded to ten nights and the names applied to these phases. Seventeen nights were given compound names and the others were given simple names.

The first phase was called the "growing large" and began with the first night of the new month with a "glimpse of the new moon." The second phase was called the "roundness" of the moon and began with the eleventh night. During this rounding phase the moon "scattered to *Akua* and descends to *Hoku* and *Mahealani.*" In the third phase the moon first "sinks" through the *laau* nights and "moves on to smallness" until the last night of the month when it is out of sight, traveling with the sun.

The Hawaiians, like many other people, thought the moon was dying during the "sinking" nights and that it spent the last night of its life in the arms of the sun renewing its life and vigor. During that night, the moon tarried with the sun in its passage through the tunnel beneath the foundations of the earth.

It was the duty of the astronomer priest to keep the record of the days and nights. He did this by counting with a set of special pebbles and stones which were shaped according to the appearance of the moon on each night of the month. The priest had a smooth rock in his temple in a safe place which was absolutely *kapu* or forbidden to anyone other than himself to touch.

Each night the astronomer watched for the coming of the moon and placed in a circle the stone shaped like the moon. He began with

Bone hooks

a splinter of a pebble for the new moon. This was followed by a series of crescent shaped pebbles, each a little fatter than the preceding until he came to the night of the full moon.

The full moon was placed at the top of the circle and indicated by a large white stone. Sinking nights were indicated by crescents. The crescents were so placed in the circle that their backs were turned toward the interior.

The last night, or dark night, was marked at the bottom of the circle by a black splintered stone. If there were only twenty-nine days in the month, the priest omitted *mauli*, the night before the last. Each month had to end with *muku* which means "out of sight" or fainting.

You can keep a moon calendar by purchasing a calendar published by some Island firm, preferably one with large squares on which the days of the month can be written.

Locate the new moon of the current month. Mark the day following it as the first of the moon month, *Hilo*. Now locate the next new moon and mark the day following it as *Hilo*.

You now have your lunar month. Fill in the days of the lunar month as follows:

1. Hilo	11. Huna	21. Olekukahi
2. Hoaka	12. Mohalu	22. Olekulua
3. Kukahi	13. Hua	23. Olepau
4. Kulua	14. Akua	24. Kaloakukahi
5. Kukolu	15. Hoku	25. Kaloakulua
6. Kupau	16. Mahealani	26. Kaloapau
7. Olekukahi	17. Kulu	27. Kane
8. Olekulua	18. Laaukukahi	28. Lono
9. Olekukolu	19. Laaukulua	29. Mauli
10. Olepau	20. Laaupau	30. Muku

Many of the Hawaiian "nights" received their names from the gods to be worshipped on those nights. The Hawaiians, having no week of seven days as we have, divided his worship days so that he went to the temple about every ten days for a series of services. He did not spend just one day in church. His services would last from one to three days. A religious man could spend one-third of his time at the temples in addition to the daily services which he held at home.

Each series of religious days were called a Kapu. The services of the third through sixth nights were the most serious and elaborate. They were the nights of the *Ku Kapu* when all men spent their time at the *heiau* (temple) of the great god *Ku* in long and tedious ceremonies.

The first night of the *Ku Kapu* (the third of the month) was named *Ku-kahi. Ku* was the name of god, and *kahi* was the number one. The second of the *Ku kapu* was *ku-lua*, the second *Ku*. The next night was *Ku-kolu*, the third. The fourth night was *Ku-pau*, the last *Ku*.

The god *Kane*, one of the four great gods of the Hawaiian, was worshipped on the twelfth and thirteenth nights in conjunction with many other lesser gods. The twelfth night was called *Mohalu* which means clearness and refers to the clearness of the rounding moon. The thirteenth night was called *Hua*. On this night the moon is rounded like an egg and therefore brings "fruitfulness."

The worship of the great god *Kanaloa* took place on the nights of the 24th, 25th and 26th. It was the *Kaloa kapu*. The nights were *Kaloa-kukahi, Kanaloa* one; *Kaloa-ku-lua, Kanaloa* two; and *Kaloa-pau, Kanaloa* finished.

The 27th and 28th nights were also *kapu*. The 27th night was *kapu* to *Kane* as the god of all living things and the 28th was *kapu* to *Lono*, the god of fertility.

Tapa beaters

There were two sets of names in each month called *ole*, nothing. Ole is the name of the wind which invariably blows during the phases of the moon which we call the first quarter and the third quarter.

The *ole* winds of the "ascending" moon prevailed four nights and we therefore have four *ole* days. They are: *Ole-kukahi* (*Ole, the* first) *Ole-kulua* (*Ole, the second*), *Olekukolu* (*Ole, the third*), and *Ole-pau* (*Ole, finished*).

The ole nights of the "descending" moon were three. They were named: *Ole-kukahi* (*Ole, the first*), *Olekulua* (*Ole, the second*) and *Ole-pau* (*Ole finished*).

The first night of the moon was called *Hilo*, to describe the narrow rim of light made by the new moon.

The second night was called *Hoaka* because the new moon became "clear" and was like an arch with points curving up on both sides like horns.

Huna, the eleventh night, means to conceal. The moon is "concealing" its horns.

Akua, the fourteenth night, reveals the fact that the moon has become a god (akua means god). It is on this night that the great round moon becomes separated from earth.

Gourd

Hoku, the fifteenth night, describes the bright moon as a star (*Hoku*-star). *Hoku* often falls on the night moderns call the full moon.

Mahealani is the 16th night of the moon and the night additionally thought of as the full moon by the Hawaiian. *Mahealani* means "where under heaven can I find room?" and to the Hawaiian signifies the great good luck and fertility of the full moon.

Kulu, the 17th night, means to drop. Water drips and the blooms of the plant drop off to show the growing fruit.

There are three *la'au* days toward the end of the month. They are the 18th, 19th and 20th. *La'au* means medicine for the sick and it also means growth in plants and trees. The days are *La'au-kukahi* (*La'au*, the first), *La'au-kulua* (*La'au*, the second) and *La'au-pau* (*La'au*, finished).

Mauli, the 29th night, means the "last breath" and describes the feeble moon which rises a little before sunrise and is seen for the last time. *Uli* also means "dark" and *ma* is the inclusive adjective which makes the word mean "All things are dark."

Muku, the last night of the lunar month, means finished or dying and describes the night as utterly dark with no moon at all.

Each night had a special significance for Hawaii's old farmers and fishermen. Each had a "calendar" of nights which were either good or bad for fishing and planting.

The dog barks, the pig squeals, the cock crows, the child cries—it is a noisy household.

* * *

While the rain is still far off, thatch your house.

* * *

A stone easily broken (a coward).

* * *

The heads of the gods are hidden in the clouds.

* * *

The little fish cannot swallow the big fish.

* * *

Eels of shallow water show their color. (An ignorant man is known by his actions.)

Sunday	Monday	Tuesday	W
	1		
	The symbol used for Sacred Nights represents a he		
6 KUKAHI	**7** KULUA	**8** KUKOLU	
	NIGHTS SACRED TO KU		
Pray	Pray	Pray	
13 OLEKUPAU Cultivate Soil Mend Gear	**14** HUNA Fishing & Planting	**15** MOHALU Sacred to Kane Planting	
20 KULU Fishing Planting Taro	**21** LA'AUKUKAHI Fishing & Planting	**22** LA'AUKULUA Fishing & Planting	LA
27 KALOAKUKAHI	**28** KALOAKULUA	**29** KALOAPAU	Sac
	SACRED TO KANALOA		
Pray Planting	Pray Planting & Fishing	Pray Fishing	

The Hawaiians reckoned time by the phases of the moon, from one new moon to the next. Theirs was a lunar calendar. On these pages a lunar month as it was observed in old Hawaii is superimposed on a present-day calendar.

HAWAIIAN CALENDAR

	Thursday	Friday	Saturday
	3	**4**	**5**
...aiian temple of worship.		**HILO**	**HOAKA** Fishing & Planting
	10	**11**	**12**
&	**OLEKUKAHI**	**OLEKULUA** Cultivate Soil Mend Gear	**OLEKUKOLU** Cultivate Soil Mend Gear
	17	**18**	**19**
□	**AKUA** Fishing & Planting	**HOKU** Fishing & Planting	**MAHEALANI** Fishing & Planting
	24	**25**	**26**
U	**OLEKUKAHI** Cultivate Soil Mend Gear	**OLEKULUA** Cultivate Soil Mend Gear	**OLEPAU** Cultivate Soil Mend Gear
	31	**1**	**2**
e	**LONO** Sacred to Lono Pray Harvest & Fishing	**MAULI** Fishing & Planting	**MURU** Dark Night

The Hawaiian calendar can thus be reckoned today by starting with the night before the new moon of any given month and marking that on a modern calendar as the first day of the month.

MOON FISHING

The fishermen of old Hawaii watched for the coming of the Pleiades stars in the east (about November 16) with as much interest as the priest who kept the calendar of religious observances or the farmer who scheduled his planting moons by the rising and setting of the Pleiades.

The fishermen hailed the appearance of the Pleiades by crying "Here come the flying fish and all the fishes of the deep ocean."

He watched the Pleiades walk through the heavens. When the stars were directly overhead (January) he knew the turtle would be coming ashore to lay its eggs.

When the Pleiades reached the "pit" of the western skies, the fisherman knew that he would do best at deep sea fishing. On the other hand, he knew that the appearance of the Pleiades in the east meant stormy weather and the abandonment of deep sea fishing.

Each moon month had a special meaning for him. He knew according to the month just what types of fish to catch and just when the fish would be at their fattest and best. This ancient knowledge of the Hawaiians still prevails today.

MAKALI'I (December-January) the closing month of the *Makahiki* (harvest festival) in most districts was apt to be a time of hunger. Food stores had often been exhausted during the feasts held in conjunction with the *Makahiki*.

The good fishing days were important to the people. The fishermen played an important role as a food provider as he brought in his catches on specified days.

Aku was the fish most favored, both for ceremonial purposes and for good eating. Because the weather was often stormy, the fishermen caught these deep sea fish about *Ko'a* which they had built undersea, often at depths of 1,200 feet.

The *Ko'a* were built by taking stones out in a canoe and dropping them at a specific point. The fish were fed regularly during the closed season and easily caught there during the stormy season.

Other fish favored during *Makalii* were the *aku, aholehole, kawakawa, kala, malolo, o'io, papio, ohua* and *uouoa*.

34

KAELO (January-February) is the month in which the ancients performed a ceremony placing a *tabu* on the taking of *aku* and opening the season for the taking of the *opelu* beginning the next month.

Kaelo was the moon during which salt water mullet made their first great run about the Islands.

It was the month in which lobster came ashore with the full moon on the high tide.

Other fish caught were the *o'io, aholehole, kala* (at their best) and *uouoa.*

KAULUA (February-March) is a moon best devoted to reef and inshore fishing because of the stormy weather. Fish caught are the *aku, o'io, uouoa,* black *ulua,* lobster and such reef fish as the *kumu* and *manini.*

Fishermen prepared special nets (seines) to catch the flying fish which would be prevalent during the coming month.

NANA (March-April) is the month to catch the flying fish at sea. Other favorites were the *au, o'io,* black *ulua, kumu, manini* and lobster.

WELO (April-May) was the moon during which the fishermen began to haul in *kawakawa* with their deep sea fish. He also caught *au, mahimahi,* black *ulua* and reef fish.

IKI'IKI (May-June) was the month in which to prepare the great surround nets for the expected runs of *opelu.*

It was the time for the *moi* to make their first great run either four or five nights after the full moon.

Poi tasted delicious with the best and fattest *malolo* of the season. Plentiful were the *au, ulua, ulaula, uhu, kawakawa* and squid.

KA'AONA (June-July) was the moon which brought the richest harvests to the fishermen. Great schools of *opelu* were caught and dried for the winter.

Moi ran after the full moon. Other fish caught in quantities were the *au, ulua, ahi, ulaula, u'u, uhu, kawakawa, maiko,* and squid.

HINAIA 'ELE'ELE (July-August) was another rich fishing moon. It was the last month in which the *moi* could be expected to run after the full moon. Fish caught were the *au, ahi, kawakawa, mahimahi, maiko, papio* and squid.

Shark teeth knives

MAHOE MUA (August-September) brings a moon of sudden storms and rough seas. The old fisherman made the best of his time during the good weather, but had to be constantly on the alert for sudden storms.

He caught *au, ahi, opelu, aweawea, awa, aawa, owama, ulua, maiko, papio, uhu,* squid and lobster.

MAHOE HOPE (September-October) was the moon during which

the fisherman and his wife put forth their greatest effort to complete their winter stores of fish and prepare for the *tabu* of the *Makahiki* season to follow.

The fishermen must also prepare great heaps of fish for the festivals of the *Makahiki*.

He caught the *au* (swordfish) which ran with the full moon of *Mahoe Hope*. Other favorites were the *ahi, awa, aawa, maiko, papio, aholehole, aweawea, owama, ulua* and lobster.

IKUWA (October-November), the month of stormy weather coincided with the opening ceremonies of the *Makahiki* on most Islands.

During the *Makahiki* a *tabu* was placed upon the sea and fishermen brought their canoes ashore and prepared to pay their taxes and take part in the festivities.

Women and children took over the fishing done that month and during the month of *Welehu*. They hunted the *o'opu*, a fresh water fish to be eaten with fern shoots, the *hinana*, spawn of the *o'opu*, the *opae*, a fresh water shrimp, and the *hihiwaiowi*, a small abalone which grew on rocks in fresh water.

Fish caught on the reefs were *aholehole, kala, papio, maiko* and the squid.

WELEHU (November-December), the moon of southerly storms, was spent by the fisherman taking part in the *Makahiki*. He played an important role on specified days at the end of the *Makahiki* when he was sent to sea to bring in fish for offerings.

The *o'io* began to spawn in *Welehu* and travel in great schools close to shore.

Other fish caught were the *aholehole, kala, papio, opelu, ohua,* lobster and the *uouoa*.

In general, there were few fresh fish for the populace and it was said "*Welehu* is the month of dirty water and the people must live on the sand crab."

Bowl

A rooster fed in the sun is stronger than one fed in the shade.

* * *

Any loafer can get shrimps when the shrimps are plentiful.

* * *

Love is better than a calabash *of poi and fish.*

* * *

It is a dog friend (fairweather friend); he shows recognition with his tail.

* * *

A single roll of taro *top is delicious if seasoned with affection. (A gift does not matter, it is the affection with which it is given).*

AUGURIES OF MOLES

A mole on a person is a telling indication of the characteristics of that person. Hawaiian priests could judge the personality of a subject by the location of the mole.

MOLE ON THE INSTEP. The mole indicates the person is lazy, one who loiters about without any serious thought of work. The person will never remain settled in one place.

MOLE ON THE TOP OF THE FOOT. This indicates a wandering, lazy man, but this man is not as lazy as the person with a mole on the instep.

MOLE BETWEEN THE FEET AND KNEES. This person is an itinerant, one who will not remain in his or her birthplace.

MOLE ON THE THIGHS indicates a migratory person with a great desire to work but one who will not stay settled in one place.

MOLE ON THE BACK indicates a selfish person who has no consideration for his relatives. He or she turns his back upon his relatives when he sees them coming and does not offer food.

MOLE ON THE BACK OF THE NECK is a sign of great strength. If the mole occurs on a man, he will be capable of bearing great physical burdens.

MOLE NEAR THE ADAM'S APPLE means a person fond of eating.

MOLE ON THE NOSE indicates a person fond of kissing.

MOLE ON THE EYELID indicates a contemptuous eye on the person of one who likes to criticise and one who is apt to covet the wife or property of his friends.

MOLE ON THE FOREHEAD is a sign of a wise person, one who is attentive in learning and righteous in his actions. That person should never hesitate to do good deeds.

MOLE ON THE CROWN OF THE HEAD is a sign of a blessed person, one who will be a learned counselor, a strict observer of the laws of the gods and one who will walk and talk with kings.

MOLE ON THE WRIST indicates a strong man who will be successful in wrestling, boxing and other games. He will be the winner of many a tournament.

MOLE ON THE LIP. That person is to be avoided, he is a tattler and fond of gossip.

MOLE ON THE PALM OF THE HAND indicates a most mischievous person, one who steals without being seen.

MOLE IN THE EYEBROW indicates an ill-natured, mean person, one who averts his eyes when he sees a friend approaching and does not offer food or drink.

LUNAR PLANTING

The farmer regulated his crops by the signs of the season, by the months and by days. Each was an important as the other.

HOOILO, the wet season (November through April) was the period in which the farmer abandoned fishing or work in the forests and "withdrew" to his house to spin *olona* for cords, work on his fishing and farming gear, repair his thatched house, make weapons, utensils and other gear. His women folk kept the fires burning, cleaned *lauhala* leaves, braided mats and made *kapa* cloth.

As soon as the rainy season abated, the farmer planted the fields which he had not been able to keep growing during the bad weather. His taro grew the year around. March was the time to get sweet potatoes into the ground in large quantities.

KAU, the hot season, was the time to finish growing crops, to harvest them and to work in the forests where hot weather crops could be grown. During the hottest part of the season, the farmer abandoned his plot of ground, moved with his family to the beach and settled down to the life of a fisherman. His wife spent her time at the beach cleaning and drying the surplus fish for the winter.

MAKALII (December-January) was known as the month of "Little Eyes" among the farmers and that was the interpretation the farmer gave to the name of the month.

The reason? Little eyes were showing on the shoots of yams, arrowroot, tumeric and other crops planted during the previous months.

During the month of *Makalii* the farmer returned to his plot from the *Makahiki* (harvest festival) and cleared his land for planting. He generally planted a small crop of quick growing sweet potatoes for the hungry months to follow.

KAELO (January-February) was "the drenching time." A farmer could not do a great deal of planting or farming during this period.

He had to live on his store of dried fish and sweet potatoes or taro. Food plants such as the arrowroot, yam, tumeric and ginger were watersoaked during *Kaelo* and did not grow.

The ginger and tumeric began to grow during the last day of the month. The arrowroot and the yam began to form during the month. A good source of food was the migrating bird which was nice and fat during Kaelo.

KAULUA (February-March). To the farmer Kaulua meant a month of "two minds" caused the alternating warmth and cold.

Farmers were of two minds, they didn't know whether to stay home or stay out. They planted *taro,* sweet potato and gourds in their lowland plots, and paper mulberry, yams, *olana* and arrowroot in the uplands.

Food is scarce during *Kaulua* unless the farmer has had the foresight to plant sweet potatoes to mature that month. To supplement last year's food stores, the farmer and his wife spend a good deal of time hunting wild food in the forest. The wise farmer often planted arrowroot, bananas and yams in the forest for just such times.

NANA (March-April) is the month of vigorous growth. Mildew, left by the rains, is gone from plants. Water left by the rain evaporates quickly, the soil is drier and there is thrifty growth in every living thing.

Quick growing sweet potatoes mature this month so that hunger is relieved. This is the month for the farmer to tend his garden by cultivating the soil, mulching and weeding.

WELO (April-May) is the month in which the earth is beautiful with the growing things. *Welo* means "tails that stand" and describes the sweet potato and yam vines spreading out in profusion.

The ohia tree blossoms, bringing a promise of fruit during the hot season. *Welo* is the month in which the farmer delights in his work.

Stirring sticks

IKIIKI (May-June) is the month of warm and sticky weather. The farmer does not mind for he is busy harvesting his crops. Food is plentiful and the farm family now make plans to trek to the beach and live camp fashion there.

In between harvesting, the men have time to hunt and prepare their fishing gear. The women make *kapa* cloth for clothing.

KAAONA (June-July) is the most fortunate month of all the year. It is a good month in which to build a house, a canoe or a surfboard. The man who looks for a wife during *Kaaona* will have luck. Marriages will be happy and produce strong children.

The farmer and his family take a vacation from farming and spend their time fishing. The women fish in pools, the men go to sea. There is great activity in salting and drying fish for winter stores.

HINAIAELEELE (July-August) is the month dark clouds, clinging to the mountains, bring heavy showers. The farmer collects the fruit

of the ohia tree and spreads dry grass and ferns on his garden patches for a mulch. Breadfruit is plentiful and all stomachs full. The farmer spends much of his time fishing and the women are busy curing the surplus catches for winter. The month takes on a dark beauty; the heavens are dark with rain clouds, the leaves are dark with maturity, fruit of every kind has grown dark.

MAHOE MUA (August-September), the first twin month, is the time when the earth and all growing things begin to look old as though they repented of their quick and luxuriant growth.

Farmers spend their time deep sea fishing. The farmers wife cures or sun dries the surplus fish. She cooks the surplus sweet potatoes, dries them in the sun and stores them for winter. Rain and wind alternate with good weather. Rough seas alternate with fine seas.

MAHOE HOPE (September-October), the second of the twin months, is like the first twin month in nature.

It is the time the farmer completes his stores for the rainy season and for the *Makahiki,* to be celebrated during the next moon month.

IKUWA (October-November) was often called the *Konohiki* moon because the farmers were required during *Ikuwa* to take their tax offerings to their chiefs (called *Konohiki*) for the *Makahiki,* which opened during this period.

The harvest festival officially lasted three to four months, but the farmers part in the festival took place in *Ikuwa* and *Welehu.* Only the chiefs and priests attended to the ceremonies which lasted four months.

Ikuwa is a month of bad storms, rough seas and high surf. It is the month when everyone spent most of the time surfing. There was "shouting" from above and shouting from below. Men shout, women shout, there is no one who is not shouting. That is the nature of the month.

WELEHU (November-December) is a cold, wet month. It is the time for southerly storms. Old folks lay their heads on the pillow or do indoor work.

Welehu was the important month of the year to the farmer in that the food he had raised and paid in taxes provided the where withall to celebrate the *Makahiki.* Men, women and children dressed in their best and participated in the great sports tournaments, the feasts and the hula festivals of the *Makahiki.*

To the farmer, the celebration was important. He believed that by giving his produce to the chiefs, priests and gods, he was acquiring a proportionate fertility for his fields. The greater the joy, the greater the fertility blessings.

FARMER'S CALENDAR

1. HILO: The morning of *Hilo,* beginning with the rising of the morning star and ending with the sun "standing overhead," is a most valuable time for planting, gourds, bananas, sugar cane, taro and sweet potatoes. The products planted on that day grow well and bear good fruit.

2. HOAKA: This day is only fair for planting.

3. KUKAHI: A good farmer of old Hawaii spent his night at the temple and did not plant.

4. KULUA: This night was also spent at the temple and there was no planting.

5. KUKOLU: (First night of the rising moon) is valueless for planting. Plants shoot up like coconuts but will not bear fruit.

6. KUPAU: Good for planting sweet potatoes which stand *ku* (upright) in the ground. After the *Ku kapu* was abolished, Hawaiian farmers found the four *Ku* days good for planting sweet potatoes. The *Ku* days are now considered good planting days.

7. OLEKUKAHI: The four *Ole* days are non-productive days. To the farmer, *ole* means "nothing."

8. OLEKULUA: A day disliked by farmers.

9. OLEKUKOLU: A nonproductive day, but good for hilling up sweet potatoes.

10. OLEPAU: Another generally nonproductive day, good for hilling up sweet potatoes. In some sections of the Islands, the windward sides, *Olepau* was considered an important planting day.

11. HUNA: A day much liked by farmers. It is well to plant gourds for the leaves will grow large and the gourds hide (huna) under them. Sweet potatoes planted on *Huna* will hide deep in their mounds.

12. MOHALU: A *kapu* night, but not one observed widely by the farmers. *Mohalu* is a valuable time to plant anything but trees. It

is particularly good for planting flowers. The farmers who wants fine sweet potatoes will cut his shoots on the night of *Mohalu* during *Nana* and *Welo* (March and April).

13. HUA: Another *kapu* night which farmers generally disregarded for they wanted to take advantage of the great good luck and blessing brought by the fulling moon. The farmer planted everything on *Hua* except trees. The plants would bear large *hua* (fruit).

14. AKUA: A moon which guarantees bearing in a *hoakua* (abundant) manner. On *Akua*, the farmer plants during the moonlight hours when the air is cool. He sleeps during the heat of the day. *Akua* is a particularly good night to plant bananas and coconuts.

15. HOKU: The great round moon of *Hoku* will bring blessings to the farmer who plants sweet potatoes and taro under its bright light. The fruit of the plants will grow *hoku-kua*, (lined up close together). *Hoku* is the night on which the farmer begins three days of weeding and mulching his *taro* patch. While working in his *taro* patch, he says a prayer to *Kanepuaa*, god of fertility.

16. MAHEALANI: The splendid moon of *Mahealani* is an excellent time for the farmer to plant produce of most any type such as sweet potatoes, *taro*, gourds, yams and flowers. Before starting his planting activities, the farmer should say a prayer to *Kanepuaa*, god of fertility. To the farmer, the name *Mahealani* means the fruits of his work would say "Where under heaven can we find room?" *Mahealani* is the second night of ceremoniously weeding the *taro* patch.

17. KULU: Another excellent night for planting and the third to complete the ceremonial weeding of the *taro* patch. Those who have banana shoots like to plant them during the night of *Kulu* for the farmer thought of the name as meaning "to drop" and applied it to his banana blossoms which he said would drop off and reveal another hand growing.

18. LA'AUKUKAHI: The first of the "growing" days, was not considered a desirable

Musical instruments

planting day for such things as sweet potatoes, melons and gourds because the plants would run to vine and the fruit would be woody or stringy. If the farmer had not completed planting his banana suckers on *Kulu*, he could safely plant them during the *La'au* days, for they would not run to vine.

19. LA'AUKULUA: The second of the La'au days was another day for planting bananas but not those plants which would run to vine. In wet districts during the dry season, farmers took advantage of the dry weather to put out sweet potato crops and considered the omens of the day good for him. He reasoned that *La'au* referred to the forests and that his crops would grow according to the saying, "The year grows as the forests" or "As the year returns, so the forests grow."

20. LA'AUPAU: The finish of the *La'au* days. Farmers in dry areas planted only bananas. Those in the wet areas planted sweet potatoes during the dry season so that they would have a quick growing crop during the "time of hunger."

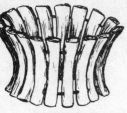

Bone bracelet

21. OLEKUKAHI: The first *Ole* day of the waning moon began a series of three days during which the farmer cultivated the soil, attended to his irrigation streams, or gathered a mulch of grass and ferns from the forests. No planting was done on an *Ole* day, for the name *Ole* means "nothing."

22. OLEKULUA. Second of the *Ole* days of the waning moon, was another day to cultivate the soil, mulch and irrigate.

23. OLEPAU: The *Ole* days finished. This is the third day spent by the farmer in cultivating the soil, mulching and irrigating.

24. KALOA KUKAHI: First of the *Kaloa* days devoted to the worship of the great god *Kanaloa,* was not generally observed as a religious day by farmers. Farmers considered the *Kaloa* days good for planting sugar cane and bamboo because the plants would grow long joints. The sugar cane would be sweet and good for making medicines. The long bamboo joints would make good containers in which to store precious articles or to carry water.

25. KALOAKULUA: Second of the *Kaloa* days *kapu* to the worship of *Kanaloa,* was another day liked by farmers to plant sugar cane and bamboo. Sugar cane was planted along the banks of the *taro* patch and grew close to the living house of the farmer. Bamboo was grown in the cool forests, often miles away from the house. Planting bamboo was a joyous occasion for the family. It provided an excursion to the mountains and a life of "camping out."

26. KALOAPAU: The finish of the *Kaloa* days was the last day for completing the planting of the sugar cane or bamboo.

27. KANE: This marked the beginning of the most important religious ceremonies of the month to the farmer, the *Kane-Lono kapu.* Since *Kane* was the great giver of life, farmers spent the night in prayer at the *Kane* temples. They prayed for life in all growing things, human beings, animals, fish, and plants. A farmer did not plant or work on the sacred day of *Kane.*

28. LONO: The second day of the *Kane-Lono kapu* was also a day to be spent in prayer. However the prayers to *Lono,* god of rain and fertility did not take up all the farmer's time. During the harvest season, *Lono* was the day favored by farmers to harvest their sweet potato crops. The day began with prayers and sacrifices to *Lono* whose

image was kept in everyman's house. At the conclusion of the religious ceremonies, the farmer and his family bathed and dressed themselves in their gayest and best. The women prepared flower *leis.*

Dressed in clean clothing and bedecked with *leis,* the head of the family went into the sweet potato patch and dug up the "best" potatoes and laid them aside to take as "first fruit" to the god *Lono* and the god *Kane.* Other first fruits were set aside for the offerings to the gods of the household. Then the family entered the patch to complete the harvest. They chanted and danced as they gathered the fruit.

After the harvest was completed, the man of the house set about the important task of cooking a pig and some of the first fruit potatoes. When cooked they were offered the gods with ceremony and then the men sat down to feast on the food in the presence of the gods.

If the farmer had no harvest to gather, he considered *Lono* one of the best days during the month to plant basic food crops. He did not forget to say prayers to *Kanepuaa,* god of fertility, for *Kanepuaa* was an incarnation of *Lono.*

29. MAULI: The "last breath" of the moon brings a good planting day. On this day at the proper season of the year, the farmer set out trees. Some trees were ornamental only. Others were the breadfruit to provide food. The farmer interpreted *Mauli* as meaning "dark" and believed trees planted on that day would grow luxuriantly with dark foliage. If the lunar month had only 29 days, then the priest who kept the calendar omitted the dark night of *Mauli.*

30. MUKU: The dark night of the "finished" or dying moon, brought a day of good planting for the farmer. He liked to plant bananas for they would grow big bunches a *"muku"* in length. The *muku* was a measure extending from the tips of the fingers on the right hand across the shoulders to the elbow of the left arm. He did not plant *taro* and sweet potato on *Muku.*

We were not taught in the same school; the noise sounds the same, but the fitness is not the same.

* * *

Water and the pounder will make the taro *into* poi *for the* calabash. *(You cannot make taro into poi by talking).*

* * *

A generous giver has nothing left in the corner. (When you have nothing to give, your friends are scarce).

44

MARCHING IN THE NIGHT

Akua, the fourteenth night of the moon when it separated from
earth and became a god, is the night all Hawaiians are on the alert for
Ka Huaka'i a ka Po, the Marchers in the Night. They are the spirits
of the dead chiefs and warriors, aumakua (guardian gods of the living) and the gods themselves.

The Hawaiian knows that the marchers are most apt to be seen
just after sunset until about sunrise. He knows that he must hide, for
to be seen by the marchers is certain death.

There are several types of Marchers. The gods may be distinguished
by a wind that blows through the forests or shrubbery. The wind
snaps off branches of great trees to clear the path for the gods.

The march of the gods is led by a row of six who carry blazing red
torches. Three of the torch carriers are females and three are males.
The sound clearly heard within their ranks is the chanting of their
names and chants of praise.

The march can be seen at great distances because the torches are so
bright. Inevitably there are thunder, lightning and a sudden down-
pour of rain and heavy surf.

Kane is the night on which the Marchers in the Night most often
consist of dead chiefs, chiefesses, priests and their close attendants.
Again, a Hawaiian conceals himself for it is death to be seen by the
Marchers.

Often the chiefs were accompanied by aumakua of the living. They
are in the march to protect any of their living children who might
be caught in the path of the march.

Many Hawaiians have seen the march of the mighty chiefs and
have been saved by their aumakua.

The dead chiefs may be carried in a manele (string hammock) just
as the chief had been carried in life. The manele creaks as it sways on
the carrying sticks.

The chief's procession are lighted by torches, but the light of the
torches is not as great as that of the gods. A warlike chief is apt to
march in the procession between two warriors.

In all these processions, a man who had held a similar position in
life, marches at the head of the column calling kapu to warn the living

to get out of the way. It is his duty to execute any living being caught in the path.

A wise Hawaiian who finds himself in the path of a procession will tear off his clothes and lie face down in the dirt hoping that by his prostration he may be saved.

These processions are most apt to be seen near the old *heiau* (temples) of ancient Hawaii.

Many Hawaiians have never seen the processions but they have heard the music of the flute, the beating of the drums and the chanting which goes on at the *heiau* at the end of a procession. Sometimes the procession of chiefs will end on a level piece of ground which in ancient days served as a place for sports tourneys. There the chiefs and attendants play their favorite old games to the loud sound of laughing and cheering.

Ancient Hawaiians knew just where the paths were located which were the favorite courses of the Marchers in the Night.

Although the favorite nights for the Marchers are *Akua* and *Kane*, Marchers have been seen during the *Ku* nights and on the nights of *Lono*.

LA'AU NIGHTS

The three nights of the La'au were the most fortunate nights of the month for the making of herb medicines by the *kahuna lapa'au* (medical man). (See the following chapter.)

Foliage was fresh and in good condition during these days. Priests in training were sent out by the *kahuna* to gather the herbs before sunrise. The gathering of herbs was a complicated ceremony said with prayers to the spirit living within the plant, to the great god *Kane*, giver of life and to the *aumakua*.

The medicines were prepared under the direction of the *kahuna* within the special house set up for him. Cleanliness and prayer were important. Each step in the preparation and mixing of the herbs was taken at the sound of special prayers said by the *kahuna*.

Hair necklace

What lay still in the calm (anger) was stirred up by the wind.

* * *

A lazy father and a lazy mother beget lazy children.

46

HAWAIIAN MEDICINE

The Hawaiian *kahuna lapa'au* (medical priest) had a pharmacopoeia of hundreds of prescriptions made up of herbs. The herbs were grown under the supervision of a priest in a special garden adjacent to a healing temple. Just how the herbs were used so effectively is still unknown. No one has yet had the Hawaiian herbs analyzed to learn their exact medical values.

But the herbs were effective and many are used today just as they were before the white man came to the Islands. For instance, a broken leg or arm can be healed if treated according to the methods of the *kahuna lapa'au*. The broken limb is first set and placed in a splint. The swelling is then reduced by applying a mass of mashed morning glory vine mixed with bark and salt.

Infections were healed by the *kahuna lapa'au* with several herbs. One method was to mash and apply a grass called *kukae puaa*. Another method was to mash the leaves of the *popolo* plant, mix them with salt and squeeze the juice into the wound.

The Hawaiian made use of practically every tree, shrub, plant, grass and the products of the sea in compounding his medicines. Sea products, such as shell fish and edible seaweed are great sources of vitamins. Minerals were obtained by the use of wood ash. Vegetable and animal products were numerous. Most prescriptions contained vitamins, minerals, vegetable and animal matter.

Popolo, a small plant of the solanum family, was the basis of the Hawaiian pharmacy. It was used in many ways for general debility, disorders of the respiratory tract, skin eruptions, and as a healing agent for cuts and wounds.

The *noni* (Morinda citrifolia) was as important as the *popolo*. The noni is a good sized bush which grows in the rainy sections of the islands. The leaves are used for "sweating out" a fever. They are crushed and applied to bruises, boils, sores and wounds. The bark is used for wounds or cuts, the juice of the roots for skin eruptions. The seeds of the fruit are also good for treating wounds. The fruit is crushed and mixed with salt or made into a drink at all stages of growth. The ripe *noni,* made into a drink, was used for heart trouble, high blood pressure and diabetes.

Probably third in importance was the use of the upland morning glory which the Hawaiian called *kowali*. It had universal uses, principally as a purgative and healer. Uses were found for every portion of the vine from the roots to the tender leaves.

These three are only a portion of the list of botanical varieties used in making up prescriptions by the *kahuna lapa'au*. They do not include many other sources of materials used for medication.

RULES FOR FISHING

Correct behavior was a serious thing with the fisherman's family of old Hawaii. If the fisherman's wife and children did not behave themselves, the fish knew it and would run away.

A woman must never at any time touch a fisherman's equipment. Therefore all rods, hooks, lines and other paraphanelia were carefully stowed away in high places in the house.

When a fisherman took down his lines or brought his nets into the house to work on them, the room in which he worked was *kapu* to women and children. Nets must never be walked over lest they get dirty and drive the fish away.

A woman should never go near a fishing canoe, lest she defile it.

When the fisherman packed up his gear and left home to go fishing, his wife never asked where he was going or made any mention of his fishing. If the husband said anything at all, he would say "I am going to the mountains." Fish have keen hearing and can overhear conversations.

During the time the husband was absent, the family were placed under a *kapu*. They could not quarrel, they could not fight, indulge in loud talk, loud games or filthy talk.

If the wife played around with a male guest while the husband was absent, the husband would know immediately. His fish hook would break or some fish which he had caught would get away before he could lift it from the water.

If the family quarreled, the fish would run from the fisherman's bait.

If they indulged in hilarious play, the fish frisked about his bait and swam away.

If the fisherman had left bait at home, the family did not dare eat it, no matter how hungry they were.

To covet the food or the property of a neighbor was also bad conduct for the fisherman's family.

It is only in modern times that women help with the fishing and pulling in nets. Ancient Hawaiian women were forbidden to come near the nets.

A woman could hunt for fish in fresh water and pools on land.

but never the sea. She could collect limpits and shell fish or *limu* (seaweed) from the rocks along the seashore. She could even wade out into tidal waters and catch fish with her hands or basket.

If the husband had a net stretched out across an inlet, the women of his family had better manners than to walk across the beach in front of the net and scare the fish with the crunching of the sand under their feet.

A fisherman never took bananas on a fishing trip and he never allowed a banana in his canoe. Bananas brought bad luck.

While fishing, the men of the party observed certain restrictions. They never talked about the fish and they never made such remarks as "here they come." The fish would overhear and turn around and swim back to sea.

If a fisherman of old Hawaii had a series of bad luck days, he knew just what to do about it.

He took a pig and all the accessories for a feast to a fishing *kahuna* and asked the *kahuna* to conduct a ceremony to overcome his bad luck.

The bad luck fisherman and his friends constructed an outdoor *lanai*, a simple structure with a roof of thatching such as sugar cane or any available material.

When the *kahuna* had the pig cooked, the fisherman and his friends gathered under the *lanai* to participate in the feast after the *kahuna* had said the prayers needed.

During the feast it was necessary for the fisherman to invite any passerby to participate in the eating. Even a dog had to be invited and fed.

After the feast was ended, all bones and scraps of fish had to be carefully gathered up and taken to the sea.

* * *

The sea has its own fragrance. (Spoken of a child of a chief by a common woman).

* * *

Fishing lure

DREAM LORE

Dreams were of utmost importance to the Hawaiian for the reason that he believed the dreams to be a visit from his personal god (*aumakua*).

It was the *aumakua's* method of giving the living person advice on how to act, a warning of possible disaster or just a friendly visit. These visits were most often made when the dreamer was falling asleep or dozing.

An interpreter of dreams was an important person in the community. The interpreter might be a gifted woman, a seer, or a priest. Dream lore was voluminous and the average person could not be expected to know all the signs or meanings of his dreams.

Often a child was named in a dream. The expectant mother might be visited by an *aumakua* and told what to name the child or a close relative of the mother might be given the name in a dream.

Dream names were important and always given the child lest it die or suffer some sort of disaster. Many stories are told of illnesses which followed when dream names were overlooked.

The following are some dreams and their interpretations.

A dreamer sees himself wearing a feather cape and a helmet on his head, symbols of the high chief.

If he is a rich man of position, the dream is a warning that he will become poor. If he is a poor man, the dream is a sign he will become rich and successful.

A dreamer sees himself flying a kite. The kite zigzags more rapidly than other kites seen in the dream. It flies high and steadily in the air.

This foretells the name of the dreamer flying into fame because of wealth beyond others. His kite is a symbol of high station.

A dreamer sees himself flying a kite. His kite moves away up high but the cord becomes entangled in the cord of another kite. His kite flies around and around and the dreamer is able to disentangle the cord so that it eventually flies free.

This dream foretells of eventual fame. The kite is a sign of his fame. The dreamer will encounter many difficulties on the way to fame, but he will eventually escape from them, just as he is able to disentangle the cord of his kite, and gain freedom from the snares set by evil doers.

A dreamer sees himself standing on the summit of a high hill. He is clad in a feather cape and helmet. He steps upon the summit and the hill flattens out under him.

The helmet and the cape are signs of royalty or chiefly power. The hill is a government position. The stepping onto the summit is a sign of victory. The leveling of the summit signifies the disappointment of those who have spoken against the dreamer in his struggle for power.

A man dreams he is encircled by a large clump of bananas. The banana clumps are heavy with fruit hanging down toward the dreamer. The bunches hanging down have secondary blossoms on the ends and the blossoms are turned toward the dreamer as though to show promise of a second bunch of bananas. The bunches on the opposite side have the blossom end turned up.

The dream means that the man, like the banana clumps, will be known on the day he bears fruit. The bananas which hang down and their blossoms are a sign of gain. The dreamer will become wealthy and his wealth will increase until the day of his death.

A dreamer sees himself standing at the base of a high cliff. Not long after, he sees the cliff falling down and he awakens in a sweat.

Uli uli

The dream means that wealth will descend upon him. The cliff which falls down is a heap of wealth.

A dreamer sees himself standing beneath a tall coconut tree loaded with fruit. He climbs the tree and knocks down the fruit.

The coconut tree, its height and fruit, are all symbols of wealth. The tree is a rich man of high position. The dreamer who climbed the tree and knocked down the fruit will gain great wealth by working under the rich man of position.

A dreamer beholds a fine *koa* tree growing tall and splendid. The great *koa* is surrounded by many other trees, so small they seem like undergrowth.

The fine *koa* tree is a rich man and the trees which surround it are like the friends which surround the rich man on the day he comes into his wealth.

51

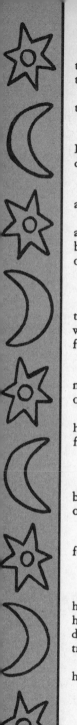

A *kahuna lapa'au* (medical man) planned to start a course of treatment for a patient on a certain day. The night before he dreamed that he saw a canoe.

Since a canoe is a bad omen, the *kahuna* postponed the day of the treatment saying he had had an unfavorable dream.

An overseer dreamed he saw a canoe being filled with freight. He awakened happy, knowing that the project planned for the next day would prosper and bring him gain.

A man went to sleep planning a fishing trip the next day. He had a dream during the night in which he saw bananas.

The fisherman stayed home the next day and mended his nets for he knew it would be useless to go fishing since he had dreamed of bananas.

A woman dreamed she had a tooth pulled.

The woman hurried to a priest to have the dream interpreted and learned that there would soon be a death in her immediate family.

Drum

A sick man was being treated for his illness by a *kahuna*. The sick man dreamed of finding a spring of fresh sweet water.

The next day he told the *kahuna* of his dream. The *kahuna* told him to rejoice, that he would surely get well since it is a good omen for the sick to dream of sweet water.

A dreamer saw a close friend going swimming in sea water.

The dream foretold the death of the friend. Had his friend gone bathing in fresh water, the dream would have foretold life. He dreamed of salt water; it foretold death.

A man dreamed he saw a house burning. In his dream, the man fought hard to put out the blaze.

The next day the dreamer had a violent quarrel with his wife.

A canoe builder had selected a nice tree in the forest to fell and hew into a canoe. The night before he placed his adz in a temple to have it blessed and slept in the temple. As he was going to sleep, he dreamed that the *elepaio* bird came to him and warned him that the trunk of the tree was rotten.

The canoe builder postponed his tree cutting, telling his men that he had dreamed an unfavorable dream.

A man stole a pig from his neighbor's pen. That night he dreamed

52

e saw a bowl of *poi* fermenting. The *poi* spilled over and the bowl
roke.

The next day the interpreter of dreams told him that his evil deed
would become known, his fame as a thief would be widespread and
hat great misfortunes would result.

The high priest of a chief who was planning war upon his neigh-
ors had a vivid dream. In his dream he saw two lights going in op-
osite directions. The one light was carried by his chief, the other by
is neighbor. Before he awakened, the light carried by his own chief
ad been extinguished.

The next day the high priest gained an audience with his chief and
dvised him to put aside his plan to wage war, saying, "you will lose
he battle."

A wrestler planned to enter a tournament and had staked all his
ossessions upon his own victory. The night before the tournament
e dreamed that he was flying a kite in competition with his wrestling
pponent. While pulling in his kite, the line broke.

The wrestler knew then that he would be defeated in his bout and
would lose all his wealth.

He may be homely, but his name is honorable.

*   *   *

A lazy beauty is fit only for the refuse pile.

*   *   *

*Like the crook in the branch of the tree, so will be the shadow of
hat branch. (If the parent is crooked, so will be the child).*

*   *   *

You are known when you have plenty.

53

COOKING METHODS

Men did the cooking in old Hawaii. A respectable head of household had a special *halau,* a shed-like structure with a roof an only one or two sides enclosed, built in his yard. In this shed he kep his cooking utensils. They included clean *lauhala* mats for the floc and the cooking pit, bowls made of hard wood, cups of gourd c coconut, porous smooth stones for heating, a hardwood stick wit which he stirred the fire, sticks for igniting a fire and a pile of firewoo

Outside the shed was his *imu,* an underground oven, with a pile c dirt beside it. There was a separate *imu* for cooking the women's foo In addition he had a shallow firepit over which he could do fast cook ing.

The head of the house did not cook three meals a day. He cooke up several days supply at one time and got the tedious job finished.

To prepare the cooking oven, he smoothed its edges, placed som of his porous rocks like a paving in the bottom and then placed hi firewood in it. This was a special process. He criss-crossed the stick so that they leaned against each other like a tent. Then he place more of his porous cooking rocks about the sticks and ignited th wood. As the wood burned, the hot rocks fell in a pattern into th bottom of his oven.

By the time the wood was consumed by the fire, the stones wer red hot and had to be handled with his hardwood stick. He carefully removed any unburnt pieces of wood so that there would be no smok to spoil the flavor of his food.

A mat of ferns, vines or big leaves such as those of the banan was now laid over the hot stones. This mat provided a clean surfac on which the food was laid and it provided vegetable matter from which steam rose to help cook the food.

The food consisted of a pig, many *taro* tubers, sweet potatoes bundles of fish and other prepared dishes.

The food was covered with a clean cooking mat and on top of the mat was placed more banana leaves and a thick covering of dirt The cooking oven was allowed to "bake" for one to three hours, depend ing upon the amount of food.

Broiled food was cooked by building a fire in the shallow pit and llowing it to die down, leaving either hot coals or charcoal. Fish or hicken was placed directly on the hot coals and allowed to broil.

Boiled food was prepared by heating a number of small porous tones in the shallow fireplace. A layer of the food (fish, chicken or greens) was placed in the bottom of a wooden bowl. A layer of stones was placed on top the food and sprinkled with clean water. Another ayer of food was placed on top the stones and then more stones. The bowl was covered with a tight lid and the food allowed to steam for a half hour or more.

KALUA PIG

First light the underground oven, then catch a pig and butcher it. Clean the pig while the oven is heating.

Remove the unburnt wood from oven and singe the hairs from he pig over the hot stones. A row of rocks placed about the edge of he oven will keep the pig from touching the earth during the process.

Scrape the skin of the pig with a sharp lava stone. Wash and sprinkle a handful of salt inside the pig. Rub the salt into the flesh and add a handful of water to make gravy.

Wet the hands and quickly stuff the pig's interior with hot stones. Make a gash under the pig's hams and rub salt in them. Then add crushed blossoms of the ginger plant. The leaves of the ginger also may be crushed and rubbed in.

Lay a blanket of banana trunks, (split open to cook quickly), add more ginger leaves and lay the pig on it. Pile *taro* and other food to be cooked about the pig. Cover all with a clean mat and pile dirt on top. Cook one and one half to three hours, depending upon size of the pig.

PA'IA'I (Hard Poi)

Pull as many *taro* plants from the patch as needed to feed the family for several days. Cut the tops from the bulb-like tuber and wash clean. Bake the *taro* in an underground oven. Open and cool. Then scrape with a sharp-edged shell or stone.

Select a cool, clean spot under a tree. Spread a mat on the ground and place the *poi*-making board (a hard wood trough-like board about three feet in length) on the mat and place beside it the *poi* pounder (stone cylinder) and a bowl of clean water. In another bowl place the peeled cooked *taro*.

Spear rack

Place one *taro* on the board and pound. Keep adding to it until all the *taro* is beaten into a heavy mass.

Grasp the poi pounder with both hands, raise it above the head and bring it down onto the *taro* with a sideway motion. Repeat this until the stone makes a double sound when it meets the mass of taro. If mixture becomes too firm to work, sprinkle a little water over it and mix in. When completed, the taro is *pa'ia'i*.

Store it in a covered calabash or wrap in clean *ti* leaves.

POI

Take a lump of *pa'ia'i* (hard poi) sufficient to make *poi* for the family for two or three days. Place it in a clean bowl which has never been used for any other purpose than to hold *poi*.

Place a bowl of clean water beside it. Knead the hard *poi* until it is pliable. Begin by punching it in the middle and knead with a motion that begins at the edge and works toward the middle.

As soon as the *poi* becomes elastic, add a little water and continue the kneading until the water is absorbed. Add a little more water sprinkling it in handfuls over the *poi*.

Reverse the kneading motion. Knead from the center out, turning the bowl with each motion. Continue adding small quantities water until the poi is of the right consistency to eat with one, two three fingers. Never allow the poi to become watery so that it sticks to the fingers.

Place the completed *poi* into a large *calabash*, cover with a lid clean ti leaves and hang high on a rack where it will keep clean.

LAULAU

Prepare a bundle of clean *ti* leaves. Take four of the leaves and flatten them out. Lay the four on top of one another in a crisscross pattern to make a plate.

Have on hand a quantity of young *taro* leaves, picked from the plant before they have uncurled. Remove the midriff from the leaves.

Lay a thick mat of the *taro* leaves on the *ti* leaves. Place several chunks of pork on top the *taro* leaves. Sprinkle with salt.

Poi pounder

Tie the *taro* leaves about the pork so that it makes a bundle. Tie the *ti* leaves about the whole. Place about a pig in the underground oven and bake.

Each *laulau* serves one person.

LUAU

Go into the *taro* patch and select young leaves to pick. The leaves should still be folded within their sheath.

Wash and tear away the cylindrical stem. Tear out the midriff.

Lay the *taro* in a wooden bowl. Place hot rocks over the leaves sprinkle with a little water, add another layer of *taro*, then stones. Cover tight and steam.

HAHA

Select the stems of the *taro* leaves, either young or old. Cut off the leaf portion and steam as above.

PUAKALO

Cut the flower cluster of the *taro* plant. Be sure to take a portion of the stem *(haha)* with the flower.

Clean by removing the stamens of the flower which have a bitter taste and cause the mouth to pucker.

Wash and place in a wooden bowl to steam as above.

DRY FISH

Opelu are the best fish to dry. As soon as the fisherman brings in the fish (caught by the boatloads) split them open and remove "innards."

Salt and hang the fish up to dry in the sun. If the weather is bad, build a fire in a small hut. Hang the fish over the smoldering fire and allow to smoke several days.

Dry fish may be served as dry fish with *poi*. They are delicious if broiled for a few minutes over hot coals.

Clock

LIMU

Pick the edible seaweed which is found growing in shallow water. Wash and clean out all sand and dirt.

Chop or pound and eat as a relish while fresh.

INIMONA

Spread a quantity of shelled *kukui* nuts upon hot coals. When thoroughly baked, place on a rock and pound. Add salt as needed.

A fine flavor may be obtained by adding a few drops of the dried ink of the squid.

Eat as a relish with either fish and *poi* or with *kalua* pig and poi.

KULOLO

Peel and grate a raw *taro*. Grate up the meat of a ripe coconut and extract the juice from it by squeezing water through the grated meat.

Mix the coconut meat and milk with the raw *taro*. Place in a covered bowl and bake with the pig in an oven.

MOHIHI AWAAWA

When the quick growing *mohihi* sweet potato is ready to harvest, call in all the neighbors and relatives. Harvest the patch.

Prepare a number of the largest bowls or containers.

Wash the sweet potatoes, chop them up and put them into the bowls. Add water to fill bowl, mash the sweet potatoes with a hard wood stick.

Cover and allow to ferment for three days. Stir with a stick each day to keep the mixture fermenting.

Serve as a refresher at a feast.

* * *

When a herd of pigs go in single file, a storm is coming.

WISE SAYINGS

The kaunaoa vine creeps above, it has no stem, its only stem the wood it creeps on. (The kaunaoa is a parasite).

* * *

Things carefully kept are not gotten at by rats.

* * *

He has gone on the narrow stranded way (death).

* * *

The bones of a bad chief will not stay hidden; the bones of a good chief will remain hidden forever.

* * *

A good surf rider will not get wet.

* * *

The mouth may talk, but keep your hands busy.

* * *

The sand crab is small but digs a deep hole.

* * *

Small knowledge moves slowly.

* * *

The eyes are blinded by the fog, making the road appear longer.

* * *

In the life of a man there is a going down, a going up and a level going.

* * *

Maui is rainless; the nose of the sun is exposed.

* * *

The Kauai men are hard (headstrong).

* * *

High are the roofs of Hanalei (high minded).

* * *

Unfriendly are the eyes of the people of Oahu. (They do not notice strangers).

* * *

The prayers of Molokai are matured. (They have come true).

* * *

A bright red district is Kalawao. (Kalawao, Lanai is hit early by the sun).

* * *

Those of Hawaii lick the ti leaf. (The greedy people of Hawaii licked the ti leaf in which the food was enclosed).

CLOUD PROPHECY

The *kilokilo* was an important person generally attached to the court of a king or to the temple of the king's high priest. He was an astronomer priest, versed in the language of the stars, who watched the formation of the clouds and the flight of the stars to determine the fate of the kingdom and the chief he served.

In fact, the fate of the kingdom depended upon the skill with which the *kilikilo* could foretell and translate the language of the stars so that the king would know how to conduct his affairs of state. If his forecasts were good, he became renowned through out the Islands as a prophet.

In making his forecasts, the prophet took into consideration the winds, the appearance of the ocean as well as the cloud formations and color and the appearance of the heavens. His knowledge was great. He had a rich vocabulary to describe the color, formation and type of each.

The prophet wrapped himself in a paper-bark garment and spent the early morning and waning hours scanning the sky, the horizon and the sea for portents.

A cloud had a special significance for him according to its shape, color and the mode of travel. A red cloud was a red eyeball, a cloud hanging low in the sky was swollen. He noted whether the cloud was sheltering in character, thick and black or threatening rain.

If a cloud was narrow and long, hanging low in the horizon, he called it a bunch or cluster. If the leaves of the cluster pointed down, it indicated rain and wind. If the leaves pointed up, there would be calm weather. If the cloud was yellowish and hung low, he called it plump and knew there would be good weather.

Black clouds gathering in the sky were the heavenly reservoir from which the rain came.

When the clouds in the eastern heavens were red in patches before sunrise, he called them *kahea,* a call, and predicted rain. If a cloud lay smooth over the mountain in the morning, it foretold rain. If the mountains were shut in with heavy clouds, it foretold a heavy rain.

If the sky was overcast with no wind, the prophet called the heavens shut up and predicted thunder, lightning and heavy rain.

If there were thunder, lightning and a rainbow with a rain, the prophet predicted a short rain. If the rain was accompanied with wind he predicted a long storm.

If in the evening, the skies were blue-black at sunset, then the prophet predicted a high surf. If there was an opening in the cloud which looked like the jaw of a sword fish, he predicted rain. If during a storm, the western skies were red at sunset, then the prophet would say, the storm is ended.

A procession of canoes seen in the clouds predicted the unexpected visit of a chief from another island. A small ring about the moon foretold the coming of large schools of fish. A large ring foretold a storm.

If the old moon were visible about the new moon, there would be a storm.

High seas with crashing surf foretold the death of a great chief.

A guardian dog deity called *Ilio* was often seen in the clouds which hung over the mountains. If the dog head could plainly be seen in the cloud and the head pointed to the west, then rain was certain to follow.

If the head pointed to the east, the weather would be fair. If during a storm the dog cloud began to break into fleecy white clouds then the prophet said "the dog of storm strips off his robe" and the people knew that the storm was ending.

The waves of the ocean are turned backward. (Two friends are not on speaking terms).

*   *   *

You will not get wet; the canoe is big.

*   *   *

He must be from the uplands, he cannot paddle. (He is awkward).

*   *   *

The water of the spring is dry, the dirt is bubbling up. (Said of a person who has no good arguments and uses abuse.)

*   *   *

A water gourd gurgles only when it is not full. (An ignorant man has plenty to say).

*   *   *

The gourd of wisdom. (Description of a wise man).

*   *   *

Do not expect anything from a dead tree, you will get nothing there.

FISHERMAN'S CALENDAR

1. HILO is a good night for fishing. The tide recedes in the evening and during the night. There is a slight rise and fall of the sea during the morning hours when it washes up the sand and restores it to the beaches. The night is calm and there is good fishing along the beaches and the reefs. Fishing is not so good during the daylight hours for the sea is rough.

2. HOAKA brings another night much like *Hilo*, but fishermen are warned to watch for shadows which the new moon casts on the water to scare away the fish.

3. KUKAHI) These four nights are not good for fishing. The nights
4. KULUA) were spent in the temple. Any fishing done occurs
5. KUKOLU) during the daylight hours before the sun stands over-
6. KUPAU) head. It is then the water is low on the reefs and the beach is crowded with fishermen.

7. OLEKUKAHI) These four nights are nonproductive and nothing
8. OLEKULUA) will be had from the sea. The Ole winds blow
9. OLEKUKOLU) and cause rough seas.
10. OLEKUPAU)

11. HUNA: The rough seas of the *Ole* days now become calm and there is good fishing during the evening and night.

12. MOHALU: Good fishermen did not fish, they spent the night in prayer. *Mohalu* begins the *Kapu* of *Hua*.

13. HUA: The tide goes out during the evening hours. Low tide prevails during the morning. The fishing is good and the smart fisherman went with his canoe to do deep sea fishing.

14. AKUA: Fishing is best at sea, but the old Hawaiian fisherman knew you could not depend upon the weather for the sea might be rough or it might be calm.

15. HOKU: A good day for deep sea fishing.

16. MAHEALANI: An excellent day for deep sea fishing.

17. KULU: Another good day for deep sea fishing. A high tide of the evening hours recedes during the night and the incoming tide gathers up the sand and restores it to the beaches bringing with the sand much seaweed.

18. LA'AUKUKAHI)   These are three days of fair fishing. A moderate
19. LA'AUKULUA)   sea on *La'au* first becomes rough by the end of
20. LA'AUPAU   )   the three days. Fishing is best at sea.

21. OLEKUKAHI)   The three *Ole* days are a signal for rough sea
22. OLEKULUA)   and poor fishing. Nothing will be had from
23. OLEPAU   )   the sea.

24. KALOAKUKAHI: The seas are still rough from the Ole winds,
so that there is poor fishing at sea.

25. KALOAKULUA: The seas begin to flatten out and there is good
fishing on the reefs and at sea.

26. KALOAPAU: A good day for reef fishing and hunting for the
shell fish. Also good for gathering limu.

27. KANE: A day and night of excellent reef fishing. Pole fishing
during the day, torch fishing at night.

28. LONO: An excellent day for pole fishing, diving and torching.

29. MAULI: Good for fishing on the reefs.

30. MUKU: A fine day for fishing offshore and on the reefs. The
tide gathers up the sand and restores it to the beaches.

STAR CHART

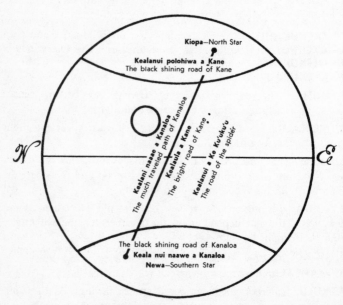

Na ala nui o hoku hookele—Highways of stars

Na hoku ai-aina—Stars which rule the land

Na hoku o ka lewa—Foreign or outside stars

KAHUNAS were the learned men of old Hawaii, specializing in various fields such as religion, medicine, and astronomy. The *kahuna* depicted here and on the cover is from an old French print, and was identified by the artist as a priest of Lono. His staff had spiritual power, as did the priest himself. His cape was made of red *tapa*.

It is burning low, the tale is on the run. (End of story).

RECOMMENDED BOOKS

Handy Hawaiian Dictionary *compiled by Henry P. Judd, Mary Kawena Pukui and John F. G. Stokes*
Scholarly and thorough, this work by the three foremost contemporary authorities on the Hawaiian language is valuable even to those who are only casually interested in learning the fewest of Hawaiian words and phrases. English-Hawaiian and Hawaiian-English dictionaries in addition to grammatical notes, an introduction to the Hawaiian alphabet and pronunciation make this book easy to understand.
4.25 in. X 7 in. • 324 pp • ISBN 1-56647-112-5 • Softcover • $4.95 • ETA Nov/Dec 1995

Hawaii This and That *by LaRue W. Piercy*
The author, a former aloha greeter at historic Mokuaikana Church in Kailua-Kona wrote this book to provide answers to the most frequently asked questions by the thousands of people from all over the world whom he met there. Here are most of the facts that make Hawai'i so grand and wonderful. A handy digest of information and background knowledge about Hawai'i's 50th state arranged for easy reference.
6 in. X 9 in. • 60pp • ISBN 1-56647-064-1 • Softcover • $4.95

Hawaii Fact and Reference: Recent and Historical Facts and Events in the Fiftieth State *by Anthony Michael Oliver*
Hawai'i's most all-encompassing reference book presents an authoritative and interesting array of facts and figures on the Islands. All the information you can possibly need. Invaluable to students, researchers and curiosity seekers.
8 in. X 10 in. • 300 pp • ISBN 1-56647-061-7 • Softcover • $12.95

ABC Hawaii: A Reference Guide—Everything to Know About the Islands *by Dr. Randall Mita, photography by Douglas Peebles*
For visitors, the ultimate way to plan, enjoy and remember your Hawai'i experience. Events, sites, scenic attractions, historical and cultural information in an easy-to-read and easy-to-find format. Detailed tours of all main islands. For locals and Kamaainas, a refresher course on what makes Hawai'i great.
6 in. X 9 in. • 208 pp • ISBN 0-935180-84-2 • Softcover • Maps • Flower guide • Glossary • 500 Photographs • $14.95

Myths and Legends of Hawaii *by Dr. W. D. Westervelt*
A broadly inclusive collection of folklore by leading authority. Completely edited for today's readers, includes the great prehistoric tales of Maui, Hina, Pele and her fiery family, and a dozen other heroic beings, human or ghostly.
4.25 in. X 7 in. • 266 pp • ISBN 0-935180-43-5 • Mass market • $4.95